WINNING

the

MOMENT

WINNING

the

MOMENT

A BLUEPRINT FOR A
NEW MINDSET AND FOCUS

CODY ADENT

Advantage | Books

Published by Advantage, Charleston, South Carolina.
Member of Advantage Media.

ADVANTAGE is a registered trademark, and the Advantage colophon is a trademark of Advantage Media Group, Inc.

Printed in the United States of America.

10 9 8 7 6 5 4 3 2 1

ISBN: 978-1-64225-562-1 (Paperback)
ISBN: 978-1-64225-561-4 (eBook)

LCCN: 2022920711

Cover design by Hampton Lamoureux.
Layout design by Wesley Strickland.

This publication is designed to provide accurate and authoritative information in regard to the subject matter covered. It is sold with the understanding that the publisher is not engaged in rendering legal, accounting, or other professional services. If legal advice or other expert assistance is required, the services of a competent professional person should be sought.

Advantage Media helps busy entrepreneurs, CEOs, and leaders write and publish a book to grow their business and become the authority in their field. Advantage authors comprise an exclusive community of industry professionals, idea-makers, and thought leaders. Do you have a book idea or manuscript for consideration? We would love to hear from you at **AdvantageMedia.com**.

I want to dedicate this book to my incredible wife, Meagan. Without her most of the stories in this book wouldn't exist, and I don't believe I would have arrived at a place to make my dream of publishing this book a reality.

My two beautiful children, Olivia and Cash, I hope this book can serve as a guide and a source of inspiration for you in your development into adulthood.

I also want to include my Dad and Mom, without their guidance and support as a child I wouldn't have learned the skills and lessons I did as a kid. It's because of them I started my journey of winning the moment.

CONTENTS

ACKNOWLEDGMENTS

To my business partner, Breck Dockstader, you created the momentum in the Universe when you called me one Sunday morning while reading the book our team was reviewing that week and said, "Everything in this book I've heard you say before, you need to write a book." The next day I was approached by my publishing company. Without those words of encouragement, I'm not sure I would have pursued the relationship. In addition to creating the spark to start the conversation, it was your motivation and support that allowed me to pursue this journey and take the time necessary to make it right. Not to mention most of the best stories in this book involve the two of us on some wild journey to make the impossible possible. I can honestly say without you this book wouldn't have been possible. You have changed my life in more ways than I can express. All of the dreams I had for myself and my family have all come true during our time working together. I couldn't be more thankful and appreciative of our partnership. Love you, brotha!

INTRODUCTION

A gangly ten-year-old shuffles away from the other kids, shoulders slumped below a sour frown. They lost the game, and it's only peewee league but might as well be the world championship. "I never should've joined the team. I don't even like playing." It could be any kid in a somewhere town playing any sport. Maybe it was you.

How did that scenario shape your relationship with winning? For many of us, the exhilaration of a win starts with childhood sports. We gravitate to the fields to join friends or simply feel accepted, playing games that are supposed to be fun and a place to cultivate skills. But if you're not athletic and losing becomes routine, pretty soon you don't want to play anymore, and you've lost that connection to winning or associate it as reserved only for others.

Money is another good example. Maybe your family didn't have much of it and you struggled making ends meet. Or perhaps you were very wealthy, but despite having all the elements of a happy life, you weren't happy. Maybe you grew up believing money is evil and your relationship with it today is contentious at best.

Sports, money, or other life components can establish unhealthy relationships to winning and prohibit your ability to succeed. I want to change that. If you love to win, you're going to love this book. If you hate winning, you're going to love this book. My goal is to change people's outlook on and relationship to winning, and losing, so they can enjoy and learn from both. I'm not here to tell you how to win or preach on a magic how-to formula for being successful— get up at 5:00 a.m. every day, don't drink alcohol, exercise twice a day, eat nuts and berries. You won't find a "What is the meaning of winning?" scripture on these pages. I'm not a sage in flowing robes on a mountain with the top ten philosophies of winning. This is about setting the tone for *yourself.* What does a win look like to you? What's a loss? If you don't want to sleep past 8:00 a.m. and got up at 7:30 today, that's a win. If you're targeting a healthier diet but gobbled a couple of cookies before bed, you didn't win but can recognize the loss and take a positive lesson into tomorrow.

I teach hospitality tourism marketing classes, and during one lecture, a student asked, "What's your key to success?"

I replied, "How do *you* define success? The key to my success is irrelevant to you because you and I likely view success differently." The first time I stepped foot in a college classroom was to teach it, and I remember telling the students, "It's a little awkward being here because you guys are asking me what to do and my first piece of advice is to go do whatever you want to do. If you want to start a popcorn business, go do it. I'd rather you get out there and fail five different times; you'll become more educated on how to start that business than sitting in this classroom all day."

My advice might be counterintuitive to those students' current intersection, but the advice doesn't change: if *X* is what you want to do, go do it.

Most people see success as an end-all, be-all, but life is linear. One student's success marker could simply be graduating college, and what he must realize is the key to his success is not the end point but how to get there. Too often, people believe life has one dramatic milestone and once they reach it, they're successful. If you reach that in your midthirties, then what? No more wins or success?

Life is a gift of many successes, not just one. What you do with them shapes who you are.

Much of our day-to-day lives is a reflection of our subconscious, which forms in childhood and shapes how we learn about winning and losing. Unfortunately, some people develop an unhealthy relationship with winning where it becomes all that matters and they must win at any cost. But it's important to remember that life is always in motion and it's not a weakness to change your mind. The world constantly evolves and becomes more informed every day; if you learn new information, you should have the ability to change your direction.

I learned to make that kind of pivot as a fourth-grade track-and-field wannabe. I loved sports but wasn't naturally good at any of them. At an annual track-and-field day, I won a sixth-place ribbon in the hurdles. There were seven people in the race. I didn't like that because I wanted to be first, but the failure was okay because it showed me that if I wanted to win, I had to do something different; I couldn't just show up next time and expect to do better. However, if I did everything I possibly could to improve and still took sixth, I'd realize I was in the wrong vertical.

I played basketball as well, and that's where my passion for winning really started. Luckily for me, my friends were all really good, so my teams were good. It felt great to win, and I knew we weren't winning because of me, but I was still a contributor. In the beginning, a win for me was just making the team. I had to bust my ass to be good enough to put on the uniform. And then once I made the team, I had to keep working hard to get some playing time and even harder to become a starter and harder still to be a captain. However, if being the best player on the team was my ultimate goal, I probably would have ended up quitting because that milestone wasn't realistic at the time. Subconsciously, I knew my talent could only go so far to being the best, and if I couldn't get there, I'd feel like a failure, but I could make the team, and that was a win for me. I just chiseled my way up to finding that success.

The same mindset ties to people's careers or diet plans or exercise regimes, if you are truly doing everything you need to be successful. The challenge is we are often dishonest with ourselves. If you're trying to eat healthier and have a bag of chips stashed in the pantry, do you dig in at night after everyone else is asleep? No one knows but you. Are you being honest with yourself?

Everyone is in different spectrums of their lives, and we don't take enough time to define for ourselves what a win is; instead, we take the easy way and let other people define it for us. That's why so many people in America are unhappy. If you buy a bigger house or fancy car, it doesn't mean you are now infinitely happy for the rest of your life. When the LA Lakers won the NBA championship, that didn't mean they never had to play again—they had to do it again the next year. Or let's say you get a promotion at work. It's a great win, but you can't sit back and think, "I've made it. I don't have to work hard anymore." You need to realize you won that moment but you're going to have to continue winning or lose your job. Wins are never definitive; you have to keep piling them up.

Most importantly, stop looking for the "I'll be happy when" moments. You'll never get there and will only succeed in sowing everyday frustration. When you reach whatever that place is where you think you'll be happy, there will be other things in life that you need or want, and that pie-in-the-sky milestone will

Stop looking for the "I'll be happy when" moments.

remain a moving target. You will also lose along the way. In fact, the human species is prone to fail, but it doesn't have to derail your momentum. We can learn from losses and recalibrate to win next time. A loss is just a loss in the moment. Don't give yourself too much credit for wins or too much heartache for losses. Everything is an opportunity to progress.

I started my first business, a cell phone store, at age nineteen; worked a second job at night; and sold the business in 2008 in my first professional pivot. I moved to a management position with a national wireless company and soon became the youngest in their history to win district manager of the year. I won the moment, but it wouldn't have happened without the tenacity to go after it. After a big win, you want to hold on to it, and it's easy to rest on your laurels, but then that benchmark becomes the new expectation, especially in sales, and you can't improve by treading water. Winning and losing requires goals and aspirations, and I continued to set new career standards in event, tourism, and hospitality management.

What does all that have to do with writing a book? Why am I here with you? Everything I'm saying has all been said by someone, somewhere. I literally have no new information. It's like how to get six-pack abs today is no different today than it was in the 1800s. We already know how to do it, but we are conditioned to believe it takes a $100-a-month gym membership to unlock the secret to a cover-model physique. That's bullshit. We all intuitively know how to be successful; we know how to be good friends and children and parents. We just have to choose to do it.

What's your catalyst to make that choice? Winning the moment is your launchpad. Here's a great example: My daughter had a birthday last week, and I wanted to wake up early that morning to spend time with her. That doesn't mean I have to choose to get up early every day for the rest of my life, but I needed, and chose to, that morning, and it was my first win of the day. I like to golf, too, and have no problem getting up at 6:30 to swing the sticks, but getting up that early to go to the gym is another story. The task of waking up is the same, but the desire for the objective is different and more difficult. I am clearly capable of dragging my butt out of bed at sunrise, but I want to do it for something I enjoy.

The path to managing this life challenge starts with recognizing who you are as an individual. If you keep missing early gym sessions, don't look at it as failing because you can't get up on time; choose a different activity. Find a form of exercise that inspires you; maybe it's mountain biking a local trail or hiking or a jog around the block. Whatever your passion, stop trying to fit into society's manufactured vision and instead, buy into what you love.

I don't have a groundbreaking new recipe for a happy life; I have a passion to help people and spark the motivation and tools to make strategic pivots to get closer to living the life they desire. This isn't a book on industry-sweeping change or a "get rich quick" prescription for entrepreneurs. It is encouragement for what can happen when you never let go of the positive. In my office one day, I realized the only thing I know is that I know nothing. I later learned that is a quote from Socrates, and that belief went on to reshape my life. The universe provides tremendous opportunity, and I want to share navigation and inspiration to grab those moments and harness their power. Call it stopping to smell the roses in a digestible package.

As a species, we have preconditioned beliefs about all facets of life that we never take the time to question. I want my message to allow you to see the world through a new lens. Being happy and fulfilled isn't difficult when you live in the now and don't set expectations. Life's challenges can derail you or become pivot points that create new opportunities or an exciting change in life direction or simply make today great. This is a blueprint for weaving a new mindset and focus into everyday life and making it the conduit to new places.

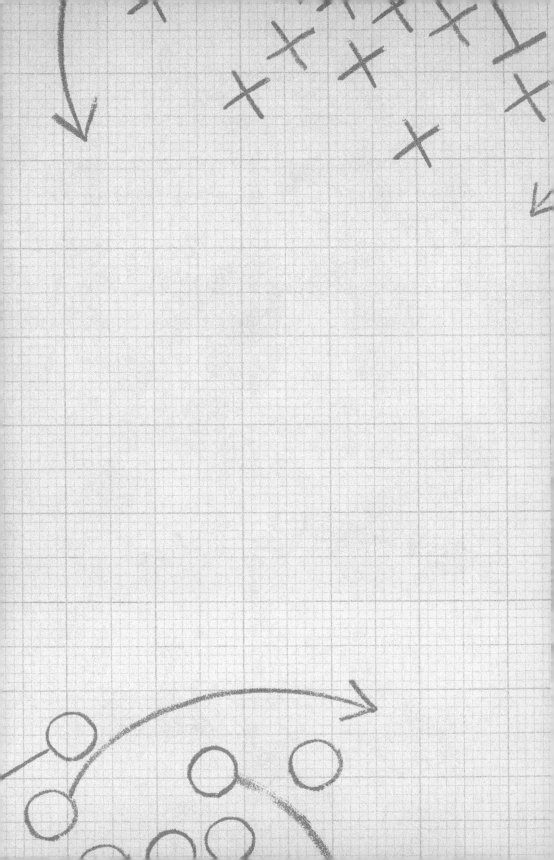

CHAPTER ONE

I KNOW NOTHING

I am the wisest man alive, for I know one thing,
and that is that I know nothing.

—PLATO

D o we really know anything with absolute certainty? If you asked me in fourth grade if the world is round or Neil Armstrong walked on the moon, my answer would be an emphatic yes to both. Today, my answer is I have no idea. I still believe both statements are true, but I don't "know" if they are. A similar conversation took place with my colleagues on diet and health. We reached the conclusion that we have no idea if a particular food or activity is good or bad for you because everyone is different and we can't possibly know the effects of long-term choices until we get to the long term.

Ultimately, who is to say what is good or bad? Most of us maintain a good/bad moral compass, but life throws a lot of curve-balls to keep things interesting. I remember a time in the early stages of building my adult life when I lost a significant chunk of money in a bad investment and compounded the loss by leveraging additional cash. I was nineteen years old, full of piss and vinegar, and a friend came to me with a "great investment idea." He'd found a Lamborghini that he could buy and flip. A sure thing, easy money. The catch: he was on parole and not allowed to leave Utah, and the car was in Texas. He just needed to use my credit card to get there (under the radar), and he'd give me $10,000 when he sold the car. I didn't trust him but did all the due diligence with a contract and everything, and sure enough, he followed through with the deal.

I was stoked. Quick and easy money. Then he did it two more times, and I was loving all the cash rolling in, but "just one more time" had me drop my guard with due diligence. I advanced him a hefty sum and found out he was essentially stringing along a Ponzi scheme. I lost all that money and was left with nothing but a scoundrel ex-friend.

It was certainly a bad experience, but the inherent lessons and growth helped mold who I am today and reinforce an acceptance that humans have a limited capacity of what we "know."

Try telling that to the fiery early-career version of me. Like most headstrong young professionals fueled with perceived invincibility, I thought I knew everything. Chief among my wisdom was the belief that success meant working sixty hours a week for the rest of my life. How else could you make a go of it and really become a career superstar? If that came at the expense of a social life, family, and physical health, so be it. And I paid that price willingly, albeit blindly.

So, is it better to log ten-hour days at the office or capitalize on shorter rounds of high-quality work? I'm not knocking long days, but is that an all-or-nothing requirement to success if the result is mediocre performance, mental and physical exhaustion, and little time with friends and family? I have a friend who's into bicycle racing and maintains top-end fitness by weaving short, intense miles into a busy work week. "I'm not training for the Tour de France," he said, "but if I can notch twenty-five miles of solid riding with intervals or hill climbs, I stay strong enough to throw down at local races and have fun keeping fit. It doesn't have to be a hundred-mile epic." He gets more benefit from focused miles, and a win for the day, without the self-imposed mental demand of "needing" to exercise five hours a day. Most importantly, he enjoys the journey without focusing only on a desired race result. Many athletes, weekend warriors or elite level, are fulfilled with only the race and crossing the finish line, and gloss over the training as mundane or simply a necessary building block. There's so much more to it!

I used to run a half marathon every year and managed to complete one full marathon, and I'm proud of that, but looking back, something was missing. I couldn't wait to take the starting line; however, with that tunnel mindset, I focused only on the objective and not the path to get there. In fact, I only enjoyed that moment when the race was over; I failed to realize the training was great too. All those runs I did to prepare, outside on my own in the fresh air and sunshine, doing something positive for my health—those were wins in their own right. It took a lot of hard work to build fitness, but I was too shortsighted to realize that with the training alone, I was racking up wins every day. Momentum was on my side, doing something I loved, and I felt healthy and energized.

Quality of life can be so much better when you tie success to accomplishments.

These examples illustrate that quality of life can be so much better when you tie success to accomplishments instead of logging time or notching a singular objective. It's far more than waiting for the next great thing as well. We do it all the time as kids, and it's easy to carry the habit as adults: Just wait till I'm sixteen and get my driver's license. Then it'll be great. Just wait until I turn twenty-one. When I get that new job. When I buy a new car. When I retire. When I'm dead.

See what I mean? I have a friend, Andrew, who is a very successful attorney with a seven-figure income, and on the surface, everything is roses. I had lunch with him one day, and he said, "Cody, I think I'm depressed." I asked why, and he replied, "I don't know … When is it going to be fun?"

I gave him a sidelong baffled look and replied, "It can be fun whenever you want it to be. You make enough money that you have the luxury of having fun whenever you want. You just choose to let the stresses and frustration of running a law firm cloud your mind in frustration instead of focusing on all the positives your job creates. It's not outside circumstances making your life not fun; it's you." He went on to explain a few scenarios, like his family still lives in a "smaller" house and he hasn't bought a new one because he's afraid that if he buys the house he wants and he's still not happy, then what? He was making everything in life definitive and tied to "the next best thing." It doesn't work that way. You can never get happiness from an outside source. Only *you* can find the happiness you want.

Sometimes, though, you muddy your own waters. Early in my career, I lived by the perception of "I'm a good leader if I'm always available. Whatever you need, just call anytime." So, I'd be on the phone at 9:00 on a Saturday night talking to staff, putting out the proverbial fires or helping them manage challenging projects. One particular evening, I was enjoying a quiet, romantic anniversary dinner with my wife at our favorite restaurant, and naturally the phone rang. Still under the spell of ubiquitous leadering, I stepped away from the table to take the call. A poor choice, given my radiant company and cozy evening vibe. On the phone was my sales associate in Tucson, mired in some kind of client problem, and I remember being frustrated with her and becoming a tad unglued. "I'm out for my anniversary dinner; why can't you figure this out?"

The situation curdled like bad yogurt, but after I cooled down, I realized she was only operating in the format I presented as appropriate and that I had essentially taken away her, and all my employees', ability to problem solve on their own. And because associates called me instead of their team managers, it also stunted the managers' ability to grow and lead their staff when I was solving all the problems. My managers were absolutely capable of handling these challenges, but they ran into a roadblock in the shape of me. The same was true with clients; I told every one of them I was available anytime, day or night. I didn't set realistic, efficient guidelines and expectations. My decisions were guided by the fear that if I didn't continue operating in that same fashion, I wouldn't be successful. A key point of that story is I could have maintained that pace and been really good at it, but only for a short time. My energy and efficiency would soon flicker and fade; you can't be that available to everyone and do it forever.

And this path isn't confined only to work life. When you offer "always-there" parameters, most people are generally keen to take you up on them. You could have a friend that seems to have a perpetual trail of life problems, and they know you're available, so they call every other day, and you always answer and listen to their troubles for an hour. But after a while, you start to dread the calls and even resent them as a person, and that's unfair to them; you never put up guardrails or even politely backed away. Instead, you opened the door to that type of relationship, but it's difficult to see it in real time because it's easier if it's someone else's fault. If we don't step back and self-diagnose our own role in successes and failures, we become part of the problem.

If you want a fulfilling work-life balance and set expectations with others accordingly, let them know you're available only weekdays from 9:00 to 5:00, if that fits your world, and they will accept it. My laptop never comes out at home anymore, and I won't take a work call after 5:00. I determined what is right and wrong for my life and set boundaries that helped establish a manageable and happy life.

Right Now Is Your Destination

Expectation is the root of disappointment. My attorney friend, Andrew, constantly expected something "better" in life instead of appreciating what he had, and because of that, he spent long periods stuck in a dismal place. Is there a clear explanation for this? I believe the single most important tool for happiness in life is living in the present, and Andrew wasn't doing it. He lived in an undefined future: I have to get my new patio done and finish the landscaping. I need to get a new TV. I need to find a new house. I'll stop working more in a few years.

He couldn't be happy because he neglected where he was *that day.* All his happiness, what he thought happiness would be, was predicated on what was in front of him. And he's not alone. For example, my assistant's friend, a successful but very busy, stress-plagued accountant, lurched into their house one day, grumbling about a looming tax deadline. He was living in a space that hadn't arrived, irritable around his family because of an unknown future. Tax deadlines are an expected part of the game anyway; why be upset right now when it changes nothing in *this* moment?

Our thoughts dictate our emotions, and we never believe *we* are making ourselves angry or sad or grumpy; it's always someone or something else's fault, but we choose to be in that state of mind because it seems easier than choosing to be happy. It's definitely not easy to consistently maintain positive thoughts, especially since we humans understand the need to exercise our bodies but neglect our minds, and that creates an imbalance. Your mind needs exercise like your body, but being positive starts with thinking positive. Consider otherworldly performances by elite athletes. Nearly all superstars incorporate yoga or meditation or other form of mind-body connection that helps them go out there and execute at the highest level.

Stating a goal out loud and referencing tangible numbers are other proven tools. A study led by psychology professor Dr. Gail Matthews at California's Dominican University revealed people are 42 percent more likely to achieve their goals if they first write them down.[1] The physical action of writing forces a clarity about what you want to achieve or where you want to be while instilling a motivation to go do it. Seeing a goal on paper right in front of you inspires strategy and questions and internal pep talks, whether you're gunning for a CEO chair or want to lose ten pounds. In fact, many renowned success stories started with the protagonist's goal in written form.

Legendary professional cyclist and three-time Tour de France winner Greg LeMond boldly and confidently, at age seventeen, wrote down his goal of winning the tour. He did it, and by the smallest margin (eight seconds) in tour history. In the same light, self-made millionaires seem to all have stories of reaching great heights after first writing down their finish line. Grant Cardone—global sales-training influencer, motivational speaker, and real estate tycoon—writes his

---

1   Peter Economy, "This Is the Way You Need to Write Down Your Goals for Faster Success," *Inc.*, February 28, 2018, https://www.inc.com/peter-economy/this-is-way-you-need-to-write-down-your-goals-for-faster-success.html.

goals twice a day, morning and night, every day. He says going to sleep to targeted goals helps them become reality. "I want to write my goals down before I go to sleep at night because they are important to me, they are valuable to me, and I get to wake up to them again tomorrow."

I enlisted a similar goal-writing strategy the year I became the leading district manager at Wireless Advocates, my first career destination. I told anyone who would listen—friends, family, coworkers, random people on the street—that my target was DM of the year, and that was one of the most powerful things I did to make it happen, with a community of support behind me. Announcing my intentions inspired the vigor to go after them; I essentially willed my goal into reality. You can also have all the trappings of a realistic goal in the numbers game. In my early career, we needed to sell a target number of cell phones each month. My first task when I went to work every day was to check my ranking. I didn't set my sights on being the best of the nine stores in my region; I wanted to be the best in the entire company. If a store in Atlanta was 2 percentage points ahead of us, I'd fire up my staff to sell X number of phones that day to beat the other guys. And that hard-target number helped us do it. The same holds true if you're trying to lose 10 pounds, bench-press 250 pounds, or save a million dollars.

So, why is this so difficult? The fact is, most people live in the past or a perceived future and miss what happens today. We dwell on a failure that upended our lives and continue to drag it along. The missed job promotion, not making the team, unlucky relationships, another weight gain. We don't allow ourselves to be in the moment and take wins that are right in front of us because we're too absorbed with the losses behind us, and that creates a negative feedback belief pendulum. I failed before; I'll fail again. Unfortunately, when you believe that, it happens.

The frustratingly fascinating game of golf is a great example. I try to hit the course with my dad a few times a week, and we turn in respectable scores, but I remember going bonkers when I first started playing. When you reach a fairway water hazard, for example, that becomes the focal point, but you don't want the ball to go there, so you start reciting an internal pep talk: *Don't hit it in the water. Don't hit it in the water.* You should be saying *Hit it on the green*, but your mind and body are focused on the obstacle, not the target, and sure enough, that 7-iron swing sends the ball right into the drink. Don't think about—don't live for—what to avoid; live for right now!

This was a sticking point for me with family vacations as well. I was always disappointed because expectations were very high, and they never lived up to the romanticized hype I created in my mind— this will be the best trip ever, the kids will be perfect angels, we'll have so much quality time together. When things didn't work out, disappointment quickly plunged the day into a somber mood. Even worse, I didn't share my lofty hopes and dreams with my wife or kids beforehand, and if a trip fell apart, everyone was crabby and it was my fault. Vacation anticipation is in fact a common affliction; we are so bad at living in the moment that we've lost the ability to enjoy the thing we set out to do. Starry-eyed dreams of the perfect trip turn into long lines, deflated dreams, and tired, crabby kids. Life-list travel to a tropical island is an especially efficient incubator of angst. You don't mind a bit getting up at 3:00 a.m. to plod through the airport or sit through a cramped multihour flight, and even languishing in customs tangles is part of the fun. You're stoked to hit the sunny beach and lounge with umbrella drinks, but eventually you have to go home, and the same travel routine becomes a living, breathing hell.

Andrew never went on vacation. I asked him, "Why don't you plan a trip and get out of town for a while with the family? You have the means to go anywhere in the world."

He said, "Great idea, but the problem is when I get there, I'm stressed about what I'm going to come back to."

I replied, "You know you're capable of handling what's in front of you and that you can overcome any issue. You couldn't have built a wildly successful law practice without that strength. No matter what happens when you're gone, you can manage it when you get back. Your firm won't sputter and fail if you leave for a week."

To glean the most satisfaction from life, focus on where you're at today.

These stories drive home the critical but oft-neglected adage that to glean the most satisfaction from life, focus on where you're at today and don't put energy into something that hasn't happened yet. My sister-in-law struggled mightily with this several years ago. She often comes to me for advice and at the time was navigating relationship issues that spiraled into a cycle of worrying about what-if events far into the future. "Will we still be together in six months? What if we're not happy anymore? Then what happens?"

My reply inspired a bewildered look. "Malissa, what are you making for dinner in six months?"

"Um, I have no idea."

"Well, it wouldn't make sense to worry about what you're having for dinner six months from now, right?"

She paused a few moments. "Yeah, I suppose."

"You can't worry about what your relationship will be like in six months either. Enjoy it today."

What will my income be next year? What will my work life look like? Will my kid make the football team? None of that gives you any value because it's not happening *now*. It's a waste of energy and time. Imagine what you could accomplish if you took all that energy you're funneling into future concerns and past failures, and focused it on what's happening in the moment.

We know nothing about tomorrow and don't need to have our entire lives figured out this minute. Appreciate the moment, focus on what's right in front of you, and don't overcommit to anything. You have the luxury and freedom to change your mind or take a different path as many times as you want. It doesn't matter if you're fifty, thirty-five, or seventy-two; you have tremendous opportunity ahead. Ray Kroc spent his career as a milkshake-device salesman before buying McDonald's at age fifty-two and turning it into the world's biggest fast-food franchise. I never thought I'd be writing this book, and I have no idea what I'll be doing in five years, but I know it'll be awesome.

Find Your Why

Our thoughts are our reality, and it's critical to protect and monitor them because we have the ability to repair, inspire, or nurture anything in our lives by changing the way we think about something or perceive a moment. If you focus on a problem and what you can do with it right now, it becomes a more manageable issue. The opposite approach, of course, creates an entirely different scenario. When you snowball a problem into "Oh, no, this might happen, and then the other thing will happen," you've created a festering, challenging obstacle. If you constantly say you'll never have money or can't lose weight or won't ever get a better job, you start to believe it and live it, subconsciously sabotaging any positive opportunities. The fact is, however, that you're already winning; you simply need to restructure your life and behave like a winner.

Phil Jackson, legendary coach of the Chicago Bulls, never stopped believing in winning. Even with multiple world titles in hand, he coached his team to stay grounded and never lose sight of their goals. Jackson had a meditation room in the Bulls' practice arena, and he made all his players visualize the games before taking the court, visualize making that shot, visualize what it feels like to win.

In our minds, we all have a version of who we want to be, and these aren't conversations we have out loud with family and friends. When you have time to think and you're hard on yourself, dissecting behaviors and feelings, that's your internal power to shape your days. What is your why? Everyone has a why, but we are all so surface level, it's hard to crack the veneer. When I have sales reps struggling, they always give me a borderline answer. It's easier and more comfortable: "Oh, you know, I'm just struggling." Well, why are you struggling? And I keep digging in because the real reason is about seven whys down. It's because they're not the person they want to be, and it's hard for people to get there, potentially because we don't want to give it time and it's a deeply intimate and personal thing. But part of winning the moment is discovering your why; otherwise, you can't have a transformative change because you're just addressing surface stuff.

An easy one is "I want to be healthier." All right, great. There's a why behind that. What are the things deep down that you want to change or accomplish that have been blocking you? Sadly, many people don't know what those things are. It takes a discovery and a rejuvenating internal conversation to get there. One of my employees, Leah, also runs a successful marketing company and had recently enrolled in additional classes at a local college. Curious, I asked her why she wanted to dive back into the lecture-homework-exam routine.

"I want to get more clients," she said.

"You have clients now."

"I know, but no one in my family ever got a college degree, and I just think it would be a good thing to do."

I asked how much the classes would cost, and if she completed the entire program, the grand total would be around $20,000. We dove into time required and opportunity costs to determine the ultimate financial outlay, and the result was staggering.

Hours sacrificed from her current company and other daily demands redirected to studies tallied $40,000. Now the degree path had a $60,000 tab. If she refocused her efforts from school to career, we realized she could land three new clients that bring in $18,000 for roughly three years each. That translates to $162,000 in opportunity costs, and all told, she'd spend $20,000 to lose out on nearly eight times that. Most importantly, why did she want to follow a plan that was counterintuitive to her objective? After talking it over, we realized she couldn't view herself as successful without a degree, but it wasn't an internal belief; it was society's vision of success. She was actively pursuing something that didn't have any value to her end goal.

"I'm only twenty-five," she said, "and I'd make my family proud by getting a degree." I admire the internal drive to make your family proud, but she didn't believe in herself, and that degree wasn't what success looked like anyway; until she learned as much, she would feel like a perpetual failure. I offered a solution that fit her scenario and personality: "We have to change your relationship and understanding of that dynamic because until we do, it doesn't matter how much money you make; you'll still feel like a failure, and that's a travesty."

"But I already spent $800 to enroll, and I won't get it back."

"It's the best investment you ever made," I said. "That $800 just netted you $162,000. You need to change your relationship with money because you're about to do something you don't really want to do, and it makes you upset to 'waste' $800." In the end, she dropped her classes and got to a place where she felt successful without outside validation. Within less than a month, she secured the first of three new clients.

What does this all mean to you? The power of your own words has tremendous influence in your life. It can create limiting beliefs or spark revolutionary change in everything from saving an extra buck to transforming a habit to notching a big promotion. You are already winning; changing the relationship with your objectives can change your life.

Knowing Nothing Is Knowing Something

Along the way in this life journey, knowledge you have and believe in today might not be the same in six months or a year, and it's important to remember that life is going to change: you'll do things differently and grow. Don't be married to anything you're doing right now because you won't do it forever, and that's okay. Many people feel lesser about themselves if they're not where they want to be today, but they don't have the vision to realize they have to be where they are right now in order to get wherever it is they're going. You can't start the journey at the finish line.

How to Get There

You already have an idea of the person you want to be. If you're not there, why hasn't it happened yet? Instead of defining goals, switch it up and identify obstacles instead. Think of five things that are prohibiting you from being who you want to be, and design a plan to conquer them. Without understanding what is sabotaging your life, the damage will only continue. Once you recognize the deterrent, it's much easier to boost your success.

Your Winning Moment

Life is wonderful and frustrating and challenging, but along the way, the universe offers gentle signs, and if we don't listen, we can miss amazing opportunities. I always wanted to write a book, but fear of failing initially held me back. It can be a tough ask to share your thoughts and philosophies with the world and know there's a chance no one will give a damn. It's easier to just not try than to try and fail, but I stuck with my goal, and the same possibilities are in your hands right now. When you have an idea of where you want to be and stay in tune with life's circumstances, you can see where your wins exist, and a big part of that is simply being present. Be here with today; it'll treat you right if you let it.

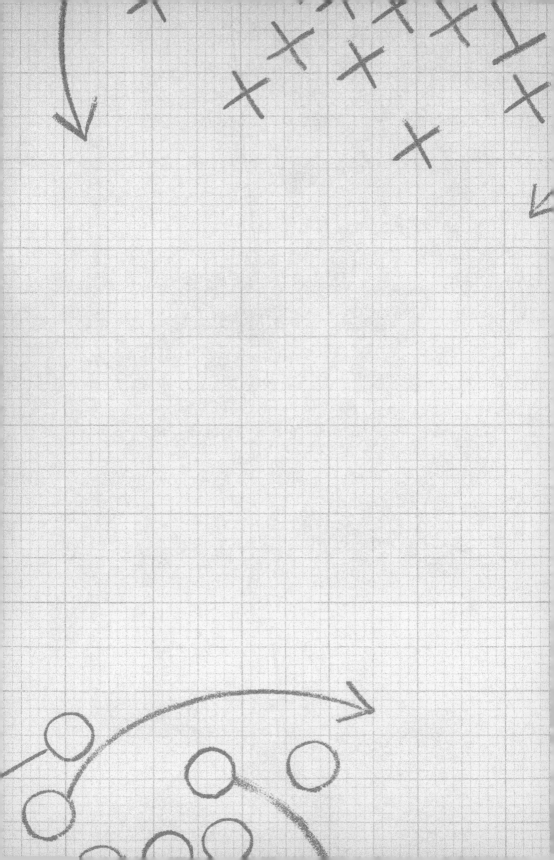

CHAPTER TWO

DON'T CHOOSE TO LOSE

I've grown most not from victories, but setbacks. If winning is God's reward, then losing is how he teaches us.

—SERENA WILLIAMS

When his parents weren't looking, a seven-year-old kid looted the kitchen pantry of its most delectable snacks and hauled them out to his red Radio Flyer wagon. He arranged the goods by category—sweet snacks up front, canned goods on the side, chips and fruit rounding out the spread—and towed the wagon up and down the street, selling pirated foodstuffs to neighbors.

I loved being that kid. The spontaneous business venture tapped my entrepreneurial spirit. (Although my parents were none too pleased when they found out I was reselling our family's sustenance.) Next up was the All-Night Midnight Bar, a sandwich-and-gift shop housed in our unfinished basement. I grew up in a great neighborhood with a lot of other kids my age, and we rode our bikes all over the place and had a wonderful time. Seeing another opportunity, I built a little makeshift store and filled it with all the toys I didn't want anymore. Then I'd put the word out: "Lunch is from noon to two. Come on over to the All-Night Midnight Bar for snacks and toys." I'd make sandwiches and offer sodas, and my "customers" could buy my old toys. The first day in business I made a little over twenty dollars, and I remember thinking while I was counting my till, "I bet I made more money than Moran (my dad's friend who owned a bar) did on his first day open." Looking back now, it's comical to think I really thought at seven years old I outsold a real business. I guess I always had that sense of belief in myself.

The streak continued with a home movie theater. We had a stack of movies, and I'd run around the neighborhood in the morning, telling my buddies about that day's lineup. "Today it's *Pet Detective* at noon and *Tommy Boy* at three," and then I'd make everyone buy tickets. I was essentially charging my friends to hang out with me!

Fun stories, all woven with the common thread that who we become as adults is a structure and reflection of our childhood more than our conscious brain understands. I didn't realize it at the time, but my pantry pilfering became part and parcel of the person I am today.

My parents were both teachers with average incomes but a great deal of stability; the quintessential middle-class household. But I always wondered if there was more to average. In my fourth-grade year, my dad left teaching and started working in our family business, introducing the roller-coaster entrepreneur dynamic to our family. We'd have a financial influx one day, and it seemed like the next, there'd be none. I learned early on that I couldn't ask for much, certainly nothing frivolous, and I saw the role money played in my parents' lives. They never really understood money's sinuous, often unpredictable path, but it had a visible bearing on their behaviors and moods—more money meant happy days, and less made them irritable. I remember them making financial decisions that, even as a young kid, I knew were doomed, and for my twenty-first birthday, all I asked for were financial books so I could learn to avoid the same scenario. I vowed never to allow money to dictate my happiness or satisfaction in life. I chose not to lose.

What does that mean? Don't choose to lose is like a real-time pep talk for winning. Let's say you're hooked on soda, and the corner convenience store has you locked in its gravitational pull like an orbiting moon. Every day on the way to work, you get sucked through the front door and walk out with an armload of chemically infused sweetness. You know it's bad for you, and you're trying to cut back to the twenty-ouncer but keep saying you'll start tomorrow. Refocus your thoughts: Your goal isn't to banish soda forever from your life; you just want to dial back the intake. Standing there at the soda fountain tomorrow will be your "don't choose to lose" moment. You've already decided you don't want to get the giant soda; you just need to follow through. It's a right-now reminder that "I don't need to do this. I can stick to my goal."

Maybe you're trying to lose weight, and every evening is a challenge. It's 9:00 p.m., and you're craving a snack. An open cupboard door reveals a stash of crackers that would be mighty tasty covered in a blanket of cheddar with some turkey slices on the side. Digging in would deliver temporary bliss but totally derail your goal. You can choose not to lose and grab a glass of water instead and walk away with a win.

I went through a related situation in first grade, where I refused to lose in order to pass a class. I had a very difficult time learning as a kid and grew up believing I was stupid because my brain's inner workings didn't line up with traditional teaching methods. Making matters worse, my first-grade teacher developed cancer, and we had a substitute the entire year; my second grade teacher's daughter got cancer, so we had a sub that year, too; and in third grade our principal passed away and my teacher became the interim principal, leaving me with another substitute. I didn't have an "official" full-time teacher until fourth grade, which didn't do my learning struggles any good, and because I couldn't retain information well, I learned certain survival skills.

I'm not proud of what happened during a first-grade spelling test, but it all ended well. A lot of us forgot to write our names on the tests, and the teacher had the anonymous papers set on a table up front. She asked us to find our test, and I knew I didn't earn a high score, but I spotted someone else's test with a perfect score, snagged it, and quickly added my name. Turned out that test belonged to the smartest girl in the class, and she ended up with mine (with a zero score). She cried, and I felt bad but had already made my decision and remained stoic in the back row. The teacher let her retake the test, and she scored 100 percent again, so that part of the story has a happy ending, and I learned as a five-year-old that if there's an opportunity in front of me to come out ahead, I'll take it.

In junior high math class, I could figure out the answers but couldn't show my work the way the teacher wanted. Every other class was the same; the teachers didn't seem to care if I actually knew the information, they just wanted to see correct answers on the paper. End grades were all that mattered: unfortunate and widespread collateral damage in traditional rote-memory teaching. It was a real challenge, and I often ended up with bad grades. I didn't make my first honor roll until the last semester of fourth grade. From that point on, I continued to get around at least a 3.5 GPA but realized I wasn't really learning any information, I was only being more skilled at gaming the system. I just thought school was not for me; I didn't see the value and ended formal education after high school graduation. I didn't believe in the education system anymore but discovered an insatiable desire for knowledge in my early twenties. I had questions I wanted answered and started collecting piles of books, thriving on learning everything I could. Reading is such a powerful tool. For example, whether or not you're a fan of Jeff Bezos, he's a brilliant individual, and reading his book is the equivalent of a four-hour conversation in his living room; you would be a fool to turn down that opportunity. And it doesn't have to be Jeff; it can be anyone who inspires you. We would never neglect an invite for a conversation with someone who inspires our desires in life, yet we constantly choose our favorite streaming service over educating ourselves—often, the excuse being that we don't have time, neglecting the fact we binge-watched the entirety of *Tiger King* over the course of two nights.

Another fascinating lesson I learned is the culmination of information from so many seasoned industry minds. I could read one financial book touting X, Y, and Z, while another title stumps for A, B, and C. It showed me there isn't one delineated way of doing things; you just need to choose what's right for you. Through it all, I realized the more I learned, there's so much I didn't know, and that's how you become the smartest person in the room—by knowing that you're not. It also taught me that if I ran into obstacles, there are tools to get around them, and an intriguing example appeared on my phone recently. A former employee of mine texted with appreciation of how I communicated and motivated her through knowledge learned from books and asked if I had suggestions to help with managing

Tools and information are out there, but so many people feel frozen.

staff. We discussed titles like *Crucial Conversations* and *Radical Candor*, compelling reads that can help fine-tune communications skills.

Tools and information are out there, but so many people feel frozen in situations with a boss or peer they can't work with or a struggling subordinate and throw up their hands and say, "I just can't work with Steve anymore," instead of being proactive with, "*How* can I work with Steve?"

I set the stage for my future by reading Robert Pringle's *The Power of Money*, which showed me how to pay off debt and utilize credit. At the time, I had no idea about the pros and cons of good debt and bad debt, but that book revealed a new horizon. My job didn't change, and I didn't make more money, but I learned how to manage it, and that created an opportunity to afford a new home and begin a new life chapter. Had I not taken the time to read the book, the dominoes wouldn't have tipped in my favor.

There's nothing more important to me than being educated and informed, but it took a long time to get here. Is this something familiar to your life as well? Childhood insecurities following you around? Channel a new mindset and realize that the way you felt as a kid, with stumbles or losses that tripped you up, doesn't mean you're destined to be a failure today.

And always, always pass on the positive to your children. Our daughter missed a full year of on-site school, like many students around the world, during the COVID pandemic. We homeschooled Liv the best we could, and when classroom teaching resumed, I knew she was falling behind because she takes after me in early-learning capacities. At the first parent-teacher conference, Liv's teachers shared that she was indeed behind on nearly every benchmark (more society-created self-esteem killers), in some cases not even to the halfway mark. Most parents in that moment are stricken with fear—"Oh my

God, my kid's a failure, what are we going to do"—but I sat there with a comfortable confidence. Yeah, it'll be hard for her for a while, with tough moments when other kids excel, but I know she'll be fine.

I understand the sinking feeling on both sides. I remember growing up and feeling lesser than my classmates because I couldn't learn as quickly or thoroughly, and in that moment, at age seven, I felt defeated and that everyone I knew was smarter than me. It wasn't a good place to be, and with Liv, my wife said we had to get a tutor or special classes. My take was yes, we'll provide extra tools, but learning will happen for her in its own time, and putting too much pressure on making it happen outside of her brain's ability will backfire and make her feel even worse and hate learning altogether. Liv has always had an incredible understanding of life, people, and conversations, with a high level of emotional intelligence. She shares my trait of troubled learning, but she also inherited my sales ability. I laugh when I watch her use little tricks to reach a desired outcome or offer advice to her aunts. Life works itself out and will let her path come; we just need to guide her. She might not be on track with what school dictates as benchmarks, but that doesn't mean she is off track; she's on her own track. She's a smart kid and will grasp that don't-lose determination in no time.

I Get Knocked Down, but I Get Up Again

I tapped Liv's same kind of grit to keep my head up hawking time-shares to make a living.

I started my first "real" job at age sixteen, working in the car-audio department at a local Best Buy. I took to it like little kids to a sledding hill and became supervisor in less than a month. A friend of mine, Breck, had worked there, too, and one day he called and said, "Cody, you have to come over and sell cell phones. I'm making great money, and you're even better at sales." Never one to shy away from an opportunity, I joined him at a CellularOne branch in Utah (moving later to Alltel), and we reveled in the go-get-'em atmosphere, interacting with customers and racking up sales. In a short time, I ranked fifteenth in sales among thousands of reps across the country, and it wasn't long before I conspired with Breck and another friend, Brian, to open our own cell phone store. We came up with a name and found a location, and Breck's dad was on board to front the initial capital.

Everything was roses, and we had plans to build and open a store in six months. Until Breck called one day and said, "Hey, man, my dad decided not to front the money. He's not comfortable with you involved with ownership." Huh? I had no idea where that came from but brushed off the rejection and told Breck it was no big deal, we'd just get a loan.

"We're not getting a loan. Sorry, but you're out."

Why did Breck's dad want me out? Or maybe he was just a scapegoat because Breck and Brian didn't want a third partner. I'll never know, but just like that, I lost my future and two best friends. It hit me hard, but the next day I got on the phone with Alltel and created a new plan—I was going solo and could start tomorrow. I named my store the Cell Phone Guy, and Alltel set me up as an authorized retailer. I found a building and had my store open in two weeks, directly across the street from my former business partners' location. I beat them to the punch and saved about $30,000 in startup costs, and they ended up moving to a competitor.

The entire scenario was a pile of stress, but I refused to be steam-rolled and let that obstacle stop me from achieving my goal. I was only nineteen, with no knowledge of running a business, so I borrowed an old version of QuickBooks from my dad and figured it out. Despite the fact that I was hanging by a financial thread, the best part of those early days was the challenge. Alltel required six months in business before I could purchase the phones on credit. Commission checks arrived only once a month, and in arrears (anything I sold in April, I didn't receive the funds for until the end of May). So, if I sold a $450 phone and the customers received the phone for free for signing up, I was out that $450 until the end of the following month, when I received my commission. That put me in a bind where I might not receive the funds to replace the device I'd just sold for sixty days! There would be times I would have only four phones in stock at any given moment. If a family of four walked in, I worked like mad to convince each of them they needed a new phone, and not just any phone but whatever four phones I had in inventory at the time. I needed more opportunity and cash flow, so I did a little research and learned I could set up a bill-paying station in my store, at no cost, which brought in a steady customer stream and earned me enough cash to buy lunch every day.

But my bills remained stubbornly persistent, and the business didn't yet make enough to pay me. Time to get a second job. In my now-hometown of St. George, Utah, we have a world-renowned Broadway-esque amphitheater, Tuacahn, that puts on riveting outdoor performances. I arranged to host a kiosk near the entrance and stocked it with those big boxes of theater candy. Behind all the Junior Mints and Twizzlers and M&M's, I had a homemade roulette wheel: just spin and win free candy! Kids couldn't resist it, and while they were spinning and picking out goodies, I had thirty seconds or so with their parents to do a time-share presentation for Wyndham. Selling a few of those would net around $200 a night, and that's what I lived on for a year. I worked open to close at the Cell Phone

Guy Monday through Saturday and nights at Tuacahn. A financial high-wire act, but I was still up there on the wire.

In April of that year, everything changed again. Alltel announced that Goldman Sachs had purchased the company. My gut told me this wouldn't end well. Goldman is an investment firm, and I knew they didn't want to run a wireless company; they'd slice off Alltel's most profitable portions and sell them to the highest bidder. I knew my future was short lived and proactively sold my branch to an investor in April of 2008, dodging the economic implosion at the last second.

I'd like to sit back and say I predicted the global economic crash, but I just didn't want to lose. When the universe hands you a sign, pay attention. It could be an opportunity for success or inspiration for a critical life pivot, and you don't want to miss it. I was in tune with events happening around me, and that made an extremely stressful, scary situation manageable. Again, being aware of signs the universe had given me, I was able to capitalize on an opportunity. The road ahead, my future, was wide open.

Don't Lose, Recalibrate

Have you ever had a preconceived notion of something you thought you knew and through experience, realized you didn't understand it at all? My bet is you have and more than once, those scenarios ended in a loss. But then what happened? Many people get a spark for a Big New Thing and march forth to do it and later realize the Big New Thing isn't right for them. They try and fail, give up, and create an internal belief that they are doomed for failure. I can't stick to the diet, I can't get up early and hit the gym, I can't get that promotion at work. And they eventually feel validated—I tried it and didn't work. Guess it's not for me. I don't have to do it anymore.

It ties back to choosing positive language. Humans don't want to fail, so it's easier to say "I don't have time to work out" than "I'm pretty happy being unfit." This is the time to step up and recalibrate. Don't choose to lose; modify the task to fit your lifestyle.

How to Get There

If you want to get up at 6:00 a.m. but it's like prying dried egg yolk from a sidewalk in July, don't attempt life-changing habit shifts every day. Turn them into a series of small victories. A bunch of little wins stacked on top of each other makes one big one. I don't know of anyone who lost twenty pounds in one day, but I know many people who lost twenty over four or five months. For your "morning person" transformation, shoot for 7:30 the first day, then 7:15. Savor your new benchmark for a couple of days, and get up fifteen minutes earlier (it's not that difficult!) until you reach your goal. You'll be amazed with the power of small wins and how they can shape your life.

Your Winning Moment

Momentum exists regardless of your decisions, so you might as well make it work in your favor. Maybe binge-watching Netflix is an obstacle to the person you want to be or you don't have the ability to recognize life obstacles or it's extremely difficult to admit to them. Whatever the case, simply being aware is a starting point for a conversation. Remember, you can't put the onus of your success on another person and use that as a crutch to dodge ownership of your future. *You* get to decide.

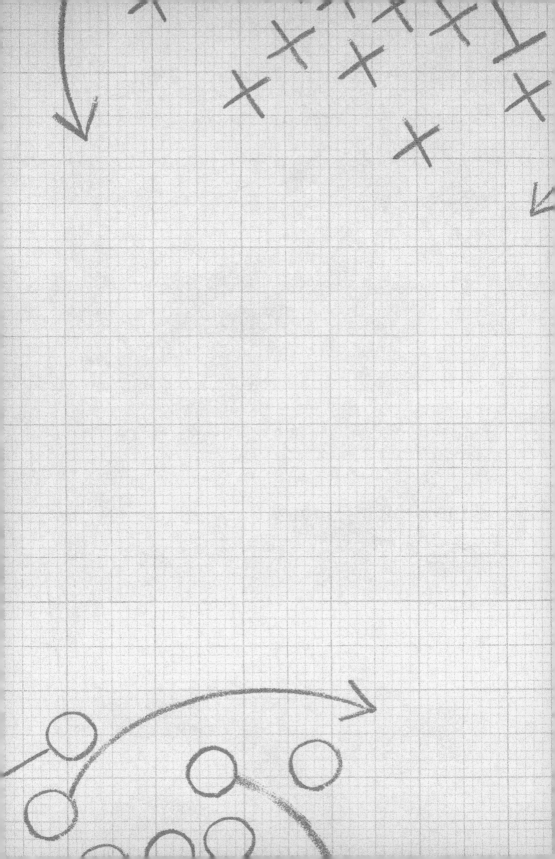

CHAPTER THREE

THE WINNER'S CIRCLE

The theme of the winner's circle is adaptability, but at the same time, staying true to your own unique frequency and that's the truth, not only in this competition but in everything in life; taking those cues from the universe—and applying them—but without losing who you are.

—RUPAUL

Would you walk away from a game of checkers after being jumped one time? Of course not. You still have eighteen pieces left and plenty of opportunities to win. But as adults, we lose sight of life's entire board. Once we mess up, we think the game is over.

It is far from over, and the best part? You can win in the midst of the action. Let's say you want to lose forty pounds. You can do it very slowly and lose ten pounds a year or condense it to six months. Neither approach is a failure, and either way, the objective is accomplished. Remember that you are a reflection of your experiences. If you want six-pack abs, work at it for three years, and still don't have them, you probably don't live a lifestyle indicative of reaching that goal. There's nothing wrong with that, but know that if you really wanted those abs, you could get 'em.

It's the little things that make the difference when shooting for a long-term goal. I remember my "get up early" challenge and lessons on interconnectedness. Fueled by Robin Sharma's *5 AM Club*, I was stoked to turn over a new workday routine. Sharma talks about the importance of starting your day before the sun, firing off with twenty minutes of movement to ignite endorphins, followed by twenty minutes of reflection and twenty minutes of learning.

I was doing okay until one day I snoozed the alarm multiple times, missing the 5:00 a.m. goal by a long shot. At the same time, I had a weight-loss target focused on not eating anything, or only vegetables, after 8:30 p.m. (Great plan, but broccoli spears aren't my favorite evening snack.) One night, I grabbed an orange but chased it with cheese and crackers. Ten minutes later I found a chocolate chip granola bar and scarfed that too. Did my snooze-alarm session that morning have an impact on my poor eating choices later? Did my subconscious "notice" that I made an exception to my goals?

I'm no behavioral scientist, but I do know that I self-sabotaged my day, an unfortunate affliction for many people in the throes of goal derailment. Remember Leah from chapter one? We talked about goals one day after work, and she said she's "never really had any goals." This sparked an interesting conversation.

"You don't have any goals because you think you're going to fail," I replied. "You have a limiting belief in your abilities and that if you set a goal, you're going to fail."

"Well, what about you? What if you wanted to be a professional golfer?"

"I wouldn't have that goal because I can't be a pro golfer at this time in my life."

"Aha, so you can't do it either," she said.

"No, I can't be a pro golfer because I have a wife and two kids and don't have the luxury of committing every day of my life to sport. But if I started today and dedicated all my time to golf, I could become a pro."

The *New Yorker* staff writer Malcolm Gladwell speaks to this type of commitment in his *Outliers* book. He says it takes about ten thousand hours to become an expert at something,[2] like me with golf clubs. Human beings can be anything they want to be—if they put in the time. And therein lies the disconnect. Today's society isn't patient or willing to fully commit to a perceived "out of reach" task, instead falling back on "I'm not musical; I can't be a world-class pianist" or "I'll never be a pro golfer because I can't make long tee shots."

Sometimes when you let yourself down with one thing, it makes it easier to do it again, and that initial failure compounds to multiple failures. You've rationalized the routine—"I failed already; it won't matter if it happens again." What really happened is you feel like a failure when in fact you simply stopped before the momentum kicked in. That's why it's so important, in whatever you're doing, to not allow yourself to stop. I remember a period of focused exercise when I had worked out thirty-two days in a row but then caught a cold and everything came to a halt. Of course, it wasn't my choice to get sick, but the brakes killed my momentum, and it took thirteen days to get going again. It was up to me to turn that wheel, and although I genuinely wanted to return to regular exercise, it was a big ask after coming to a full stop. Think about that for a minute: If you did four-week bursts of any kind of activity—work, personal, exercise—and then stopped for two weeks, that translates to sixty-three lost days over the course of a year. Simply from loss of momentum.

---

2   Malcolm Gladwell, *Outliers* (New York: Little, Brown and Company, 2008), 35.

The typical office work environment is another example. A computer sits on a desk (or even worse, accompanies workers everywhere they go in mobile devices), attracting emails all day long, like flies to a wet dog. In today's world, inboxes are often a reflection of our work and responsibilities: visual reminders of stuff we have to do. All those emails want attention, and if a hundred of them pile up, it quickly feels overwhelming to ever get through them all. You neglect them, and then senders (or your boss) start thinking you're incompetent because you haven't responded. But it's not that you can't respond to one particular email; it's trying to respond to one hundred. In the end, however, the solution is simply to start sifting through those emails, kick in momentum, and keep it rolling until you're done.

Leah and I bantered back and forth awhile longer and circled back to inspiration on momentum I gleaned from Jim Collins in *Turning the Flywheel*.[3] He discusses the transformative concept of continuously pushing a huge, heavy wheel that's difficult to get turning, but once it's up to speed in a targeted direction, you reach a point of breakthrough.

You can be whatever you want in life. Do whatever you want to do, look how you want to look, live anywhere you want—if you put in the work and give your goals the appreciation and understanding they deserve. Essentially, you can experience a single event in two ways:

➡ Walk away with a better understanding of your goal, and if it doesn't align, move forward in life, building on a positive, happy experience.

➡ Stay weighted under an "I fail at everything" mindset. Tried everything, couldn't do it, not going to try again.

---

3   Jim Collins, *Turning the Flywheel: A Monograph to Accompany Good to Great* (New York: Harper Business, 2019).

The human brain knows its host wants to be right about things, and our subconscious will always tell us we're great, whether or not it's true, so we feel good about ourselves. However, if you vocalize a propensity to fail, when given the next opportunity to succeed or fail, your subconscious is on board with "I always fail." Logically, you'd never stop yourself from doing something you want, but our bodies aren't controlled by logic; subconscious rules the day. Keep vocalizing that you're a failure and your subconscious will deliver in kind, creating a negative feedback loop. Until you break that loop, you will perpetually fail without even realizing *you* are the reason it's happening. Once you recognize the self-imposed mire, you can take away its power, and it won't take five years or ten or twenty. That's the beauty of the human mind. You can change it right now.

China or Bust

I could've changed my mind the day I boarded a plane to China. "Now boarding all seats, all rows" was my last chance to bail out. I could accept failure or punch it in the face and win. The decision would shape the next chapter of my life.

I pulled off a grand performance of hiding that I was nervous as hell. You can't exactly have a change of heart at thirty thousand feet and ask the pilot to turn the plane around. My internal pressure cooker was pegged, but I tempered it with a winning mindset. Would it work? Next thing I knew, we were at cruising altitude. In the seat next to me was my high school buddy and business partner, Breck (the same one who kicked me out of our cell phone partnership). Thirty years ago, his dad had

I could accept failure or punch it in the face and win.

41

established the Cliffrose Lodge in Utah's Zion National Park, which became Zion's premier luxury resort. It had been family operated since its inception; Breck assumed management in 2010, and today, the Cliffrose is one of the world's finest travel destinations.

Prior to Cliffrose's ascension, there were no four-star accommodations in southern Utah, including all Zion. A Tripadvisor-searching consumer in Chicago or Dallas or Spokane would see the Cliffrose as a three-star property, nothing different from an everyday Holiday Inn, and as far as they knew, the experience would be the same. AAA ratings presented a similar obstacle with archaic ratings that didn't delineate significant property contrasts. We could sink $10 million into renovations and still end up with the same ratings. The gamble wasn't worth the effort. Making matters worse, the Cliffrose is located along a national park border and, as such, is subject to all manner of restrictions on what you can and can't do. Our opportunity for growth existed only in room revenue, but we didn't have the luxury of adding more rooms or activities.

We needed to join a national brand hosting categories for unique properties, like Marriott's Autograph and Hilton's Curio, where the hotel is the hero, while the big names provide background reassurance that you'll receive everything you've come to expect from them. We chose the Hilton route, and everyone in the industry thought we were idiots and just selling out. Undeterred, we secured bank approval for renovations and, in November, renovated the original building to the studs while demolishing another building with the goal of having the new property ready by March.

One critical Hilton requirement for new properties is their approval of an exact room replica, so we connected with sources in China to build a room. With Chinese New Year rapidly approaching, the only way to make deadline was to build the room replica in a Chinese warehouse and complete the furniture order before the national holiday, and that meant Breck and I had to fly over there, purchase a million dollars in furniture, and ensure it all got done. A big trip, laced with uncertainty, but straightforward enough. We were excited, leaving for China the next day to put the cherry on top of everything we'd been working for. What could possibly go wrong?

While we were stuck in six-lane traffic on the way to the Chinese consulate in Los Angeles for visas, our bank called and said they had withdrawn from financing the project. Say what? They'd already committed, and the possibility of backing out wasn't even a distant thought on our radar: Breck's family had been working with this bank for over thirty years. Breck's face turned ghostly pale; his two siblings trusted him to follow through for their family. Our staff of fifty plus were counting on us for their livelihoods and food on the table. I felt like I was going to vomit out the window all over the 405 freeway. We hadn't just lost the opportunity to renovate the Cliffrose property; with no money to even restore it to its predemolition state, we might have ruined it forever.

A couple of hotly stressful hours later, we were sitting in our car in front of the consulate, dangling over the rim of a precipice with no lifeline. We had leveraged everything we had on the project and bought the flights with a credit card, and all we had was a demolished building in Utah to show for it. Breck turned to me with a desperate look. "What are we going to do? Should we even get on that plane tomorrow?"

It was one of those moments. We could give up and go home or stay true to our dream, dangling as it was above that ink-black void of other vanquished entrepreneurs.

"We have to do it," I said. "We're too far along. There's an institution out there that will give us the money. We have to go get this deal done. We can't give up."

And we didn't. On a handshake deal with a foreign manufacturer, with no definitive way to pay them, we built the trust we needed and shepherded the project to fruition. Our manufacturer started our $1 million furniture order with no guaranty of payment other than our word. Instead of giving in to failure, we won the moment, and the Cliffrose became the number one–ranked Hilton Curio property in the United States.

This story matters because the point is not about jetting around the globe to land a multimillion-dollar deal; it's about winning. We all have times in our lives when quitting seems easier, but I want you to change that mindset. Don't. Ever. Stop. Everything is possible if you keep moving forward.

Inspire Desire

Goals are powerful incentives with the chops to spur dramatic life change. And they often work best in visual or physical daily reminders to build strength and momentum to make impactful decisions. Being *present* in your day makes it so much more possible to maintain a positive lifestyle and inspire great things. The key is to see the little wins on the way to big ones. Sounds simple enough, but let's look closer at a "winning the moment" day.

If you're a snooze button offender but today you beat the alarm clock and got in twenty minutes of cardio before breakfast, it's a win. Standing in front of the vending machine in the office break room, you decide not to have the sugar-packed soda. That exercise of willpower is a win. Your choice of healthy foods over beer and pizza at dinner is a win.

But how do you translate this new behavior into decisions throughout the day? Ideas percolated in my head over the years but always circled back to one prevalent driver: be visual! Remember those yellow Livestrong bracelets, adorning wrists around the world in the early 1990s? Prior to his doping scandal and plummet from grace, former pro cyclist Lance Armstrong leveraged his celebrity to turn yellow rubber bracelets into a badge of honor, inspiration for cancer patients and active lifestyles, and a global symbol for winning the day. People wore the bracelets with pride, believing in their message, a part of something that made a difference.

I believed in it too. The Livestrong bracelets reminded me of my relationship with winning and its influence on how I view goals as wins and losses today. I mentioned my love of sports earlier in the book and should clarify that my relationship with winning was more one of participating. My earliest childhood memories revolve around sports. They're all I did. My parents took me to the Colorado Rockies' first major-league game, and I was hooked. In second grade, I played soccer, baseball, and basketball, and my dad coached for all of them, instilling a competitive streak I carry to this day. As a kid, I actively participated in games or practice seven days a week, in our hometown or outstate locations on traveling teams.

Among lessons in fundamentals of batting swings or free throw technique, I also learned the value of commitment. One fine summer weekend, my baseball team had a game scheduled, but my family was on a camping trip three hours away from the stadium. Keep in mind that I wasn't a great player by any means. Not even sort of good. In fact, I was terrible. But I loved to play, and my devoted parents woke me before sunrise for the long drive to the stadium. Ten minutes after arriving, league officials announced they were canceling the game due to poor field condition. Ruts in the infield, divots in the outfield, and other terrestrial maladies.

My dad would have none of it. "No way. We didn't drive three hours for nothing. There are twenty-four kids here; let's put 'em to work." And just like that, a bunch of seven-year-olds scurried back and forth like oversize ants, pulling sand graders and running baselines to compact the dirt. After the impromptu landscaping, the game went off without a hitch, and I learned the value of commitment right there in the batter's box. When you commit to something, you have to see it through, even when it seems easier to give up.

> *When you commit to something, you have to see it through, even when it seems easier to give up.*

Though I was hardly a household name on the Utah amateur athletic scene, my tenure nevertheless molded a desire to compete and win. Without natural talent, I had to work harder, and the games engaged me and made it fun. Even now, when we just play pickup basketball games, you better believe I want to win, even though we're out there more for exercise than competition. At this point in my life, if I lace up my sneakers, I damn sure want to be on the winning side at the end of the night. In 2019, in the midst of a spell of life doldrums, an idea coalesced and tapped me on the shoulder. *This.*

Here's an easily digestible illustration of where my mind was at. If your boss says, "I need you at the office at 6:00 a.m. tomorrow," you'll be there, as would most any other cognizant employee interested in a paycheck. On the other hand, if it's a matter of being at the gym by 6:00 a.m., it's tougher to hold that same commitment, and what it comes down to is we aren't willing to give ourselves the same respect we give others. I know if I have a professional task or goal in front of me, a deliverable to a manager or client, I'll never miss it. But if I tell *myself* I need to do *X*, I'm lucky if I accomplish it 25 percent of the time. No gym partner waiting for me for a sunrise workout? I'm hitting the snooze button.

So, how do we fix this ball-and-chain habit of not showing up for ourselves? I realized I needed to create a way to show up for myself and do all the things I wanted to do, be the person I wanted to be—exercise at least forty-five minutes a day, four times a week; read every day; drink alcohol only twice a week; meditate. With so many moments of choosing not to lose, not giving up, winning whenever I could, and then expounding on it all to everyone around me, I knew something special was brewing. A big part of winning, of course, is the enjoyment of it all. To help channel inner motivation, I created a simple Excel spreadsheet with categories for mind and body care. I updated it every day with green "wins" or red "losses" associated with each category, and it quickly became a momentum-building game. Naturally I wanted to see more green on the board, and that fueled an extraordinary year: I lost forty pounds, looked good, and felt great. I did a LinkedIn post with before-and-after photos and ended up with more than two hundred thousand views from people around the world with similar life dynamics.

When COVID-19 disrupted the world in 2020, I fell out of routine and realized I was making a bunch of little negative-impact decisions throughout the day. It was throwing me off my game; one bad decision fueled "permission" to make another one, and it snowballed into a day of downers. One hiccup with my win-loss spreadsheet and similar motivational tools is their visual form. You look at it once, usually in the morning, and then forget about it. I needed that visual reminder with me all day. Think about how many decisions you make on any given day and how many times the pendulum can shift one way (win) or the wrong way (lose). At the time, I had been researching willpower and its tendency to dissipate over the course of a day, a feeling I knew all too well. I typically make good decisions on the front end of a day, but right around 9:00 p.m. everything falls apart. That's when I pour a shot of whiskey or sneak a turkey sandwich and cookies or watch a half-dozen Netflix episodes of whatever. Next thing I know, it's 1:00 a.m. and I have a gut full of trouble and a tapioca brain.

The trajectory of it all fascinated me. Consider Mark Zuckerberg's routine of wearing the same clothes every day. He understands that humans are capable of only a finite number of good decisions in a day; for him, wearing the same outfit is one less decision to make, freeing up valuable brain space for more fulfilling tasks. In my case, my conscious, fully powered mind would never get up at 8:00 a.m. and throw back a couple of shots, eat a dozen cookies, or sit in front of the TV for hours. But late at night when I'm exhausted, it's easy to make "comfort food" decisions, and many of them have ripple effects the following day. Now I'm hungover, tired, and steadily gaining weight. The day is subpar, and then when evening rolls around again, I'm thinking, "Well, this day sucked anyway; no point in working out, so might as well have a drink." And so begins the negative feedback loop.

Essentially, it took me a year to build a pattern of good habits, and COVID-infused demotivation ruined it in a month. For me, it seems to take four times longer to launch good habits than to break a bad one—four days a week in the gym followed by one day skipping it means I might not make it back there for two weeks. I needed *something* to help my angel-and-devil skirmishes because the devil kept winning. "It's Thursday, close enough to Friday … go ahead and have a drink. You don't really want to go to the gym; dig into that leftover ice cream." And so on. How do we beat that? How do we show up for ourselves and maintain good-decision momentum? Vision.

If I had ten slender bracelets on my left wrist, I could create a self-prescribed, and fun, motivational challenge. Let's say I dread getting up early to go to the gym but made it there by 7:00 a.m. today. I move one bracelet to my right wrist as a victory salute and tangible reminder of my win. If I want to drink less soda, and turn my back on the vending machine, I move another bracelet. The action of moving the bracelets creates a dopamine hit, and now I have momentum behind me. Eight bracelets left; where else can I grab a win? Move all ten to the right wrist, and I win the day.

It's like a personal, mobile trainer, without barking "five more reps" at you all day, and it becomes a game to keep getting wins. If you get that first one by getting up early, it sparks a full day of internal competition. You don't want to lose and have to remove a bracelet from the success hand and move it back, right? Now you have a physical incentive to skip drinking a midday soda, and another fun part of this is it can become a challenge with others. At work or the gym or walking down the street, people will ask why you have a collection of bracelets on your wrist. It starts a conversation and sparks friendly competition. Can you move all ten bracelets to the success side before the guy in the next cubicle? If your neighbor sees you have only two bracelets left, she offers a go-get-'em adrenaline boost. Maybe your office team coordinates a contest—whichever department earns the most wins by Friday gets a catered lunch. Before long, there's a lively community of people helping each other get their wins.

The core of the bracelet challenge is it makes every decision easier but you have to do it for yourself. Far too often, people feel compelled to do things for others instead of putting themselves first.

In fact, many people are more successful in their career objectives than personal objectives. While successful people generally carry the same habits in different parts of their lives, sadly, a host of the professionally successful fail at personal goals.

We tend to let ourselves down more than pick ourselves up, but it doesn't have to be that way. It's time to run the checkerboard and do it for *you*.

What's in Your Way?

What's stopping you from being the person you want to be? That's a difficult and sometimes scary question to answer for many people and often related as simply "I don't know." But I believe what they do know are the things they *don't* want to do: Why do I keep doing that? Why do I keep skipping the gym? Why do I keep drinking late at night? Smoking weed? Gobbling cookies?

There are ten times during the day when all of us can make better decisions, and I'm not going to tell you what they are. This isn't a book of top-ten lists to salvation, and lists like that are subjective at best. *You* know the best decisions at the best times. You'll feel it organically, like the first time you wear your win-the-moment bracelets and walk into the office break room to find a mini Snickers adorned in seductive brown dress. In the grand scheme of your life over the next few decades, giving in to Snickers temptation means nothing, but for your goal right there in that moment, it's everything. Resist the chocolaty desire and move a bracelet to your winning hand, and you get the same dopamine hit you would've had from taking a bite. You're replacing a negative, temporary dopamine hit (one minute of bliss) followed by regret (damn, I wish I wouldn't have eaten that thing) with a positive decision that impacts your life.

Going through your day with confidence to know a good decision when you see it allows focus to shift to something with clear substance: avoiding obstacles. Maybe you can't turn on Netflix after 9:00 p.m. because you'll sit there for three hours. A bowl of M&M's on your desk gets the best of you every day? Remove it. You can't stop at the gas station on the way to anywhere because you know you'll buy a huge soda. Maybe you can't call Aaron or Lisa so often because you'll be stuck on the phone for an hour. You can't leave your phone within reach at work or you'll pick it up and scroll Instagram. There could be any number of detractors throughout the day; eliminating them is a potent strategy for winning those ten daily good-decision times, and the bracelets are your rocket fuel. When faced with a difficult moment and previously a lack of willpower, now you have something to lead the way to the high side of a day.

Let's think about this from a time perspective. The amount of time humans waste in their lives is staggering. Nauseating, in many respects. The social media time vacuum alone sucks up big chunks of an otherwise productive day. Long lunch hours, napping, watching TV, general farting around. My unofficial research shows the average person wastes around three hours every day, every week. Author Jay Shetty[4] tells us that over a lifetime, humans spend eleven years in front of an electronic screen for personal enjoyment. Eleven years! But if you've dialed in a win-the-moment practice that gives you the same satisfaction as time-wasting decisions, you reverse the trend. You take back enough time to give yourself an *entire additional day* every week. What could you do with an extra day on your hands?

---

4   Jay Shetty, *Think like a Monk* (New York: Simon & Schuster, 2020).

Win the Day

What's a win you've always wanted in your life but haven't been able to achieve? Everyone has something, and when you don't take the time to appreciate things, you forget how good it feels to be the person you want to be. A three-month break from the gym, for example, makes you forget how great you feel with regular exercise. Today, don't allow your focus to be only on major tasks in front of you. All choices and decisions are interconnected and controlled by your subconscious. The smallest, seemingly innocent, of choices can have a major impact on your day. Make that impact a win.

How to Get There

Start building small, positive habits daily. Be impeccable with your decision-making to the smallest detail. Stay true to your focus and goals in all aspects of your day, regardless of size or impact in your routine. Incredible growth and great success start today. You don't need to jump back into a six-day training regime; just go to the gym today. Walk around the block one time this week. If you don't read five books a week anymore, start with just ten pages today. Choose something you love to do that you've neglected, and do it for you.

Start building small, positive habits daily.

Too often, people forget they have autonomy over their life. If you think your life sucks, you have no one to blame but yourself. But no one wants to hear "change your life and create some time for fun." We don't consciously desire a crappy life, and it's easier to blame someone else: it's my boss, mother-in-law, wife, husband. Cut out toxic relationships (or smooth them over) and surround yourself with people and things you love. Channel that unfettered joy you had as a kid. If you're not having fun, what's the point?

Your Winning Moment

Don't get caught up in society's definition of success. Winning the moment is about creating a path to enjoy a fulfilling life. My sister wanted to be a vet and tried college, but it didn't work, and she feels like a failure because she's trying to fit into "this is what you have to do" instead of doing what makes *her* happy. Too many people spend too much time searching for what they "should" be doing versus what they want to do. You own it. Make it what you want.

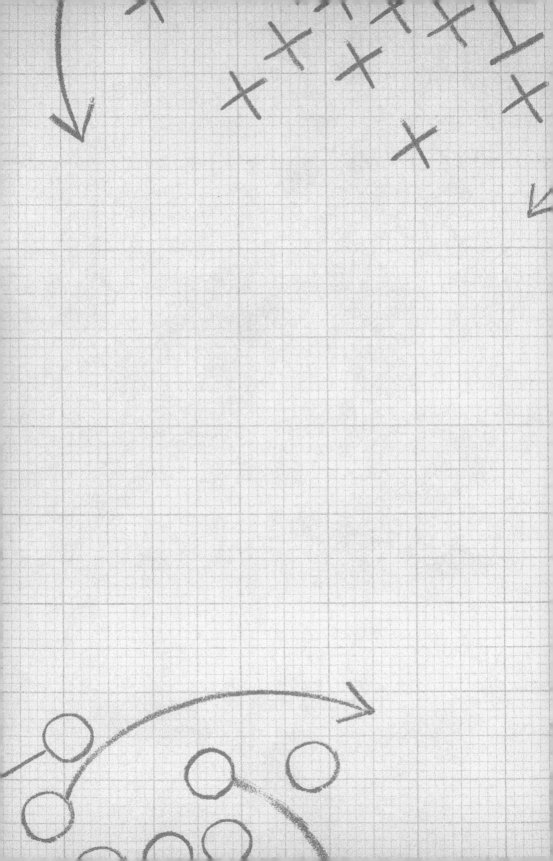

CHAPTER FOUR

IT'S ABOUT THE JOURNEY

Success is not final, failure is not fatal: it is the
courage to continue that counts.
—WINSTON CHURCHILL

What does a journey look like to you? Does it conjure images of a grizzled vagabond with a long, tormented beard and threadbare backpack hiking into the woods? A family road trip to Disneyland—three fidgety kids and fourteen hours of car time? Mountaineers' hiking to and up Mount Everest is a journey, as is simply walking around the block for some people. You could be on a journey to lose twenty pounds or run an extra five miles by the end of next month.

Whatever your passion, a journey is about understanding and finding joy in the things we do, in the moment, and not looking only to the outcome. When I was younger, all I wanted was to be successful; that single goal drove everything I did in life. I thought there was a place at which you could arrive that looked like and felt like and signified success, but I later realized that is an impossible destination. When I won District Manager of the Year as a young professional executive, that success was only temporary. I got an award at a fancy dinner presentation, and that night I got to say I was DM of the year, but it didn't mean anything once that year was over. I had no grasp of the journey and didn't appreciate its moments while they were happening; I was focused only on the brass ring.

The old "life is a journey, not a destination" adage is as powerful in its lesson as its brevity. We have a very short, beautiful, and *vibrant* time here that provides countless moments of an ultimate journey. But it moves so fast it can be difficult to savor those occasions, to allow ourselves a moment of reflection. Let's give this some perspective: it's not like you have to spend twenty minutes of alone time appreciating that you didn't guzzle a forty-ounce soda, but a few seconds to move a win-the-moment bracelet to the other hand or simply recognizing what you accomplished goes a long way.

I went through a similar scenario after moving into our new home. I saw only the finished product in front of me: having everything just how I wanted it, setting up my office, getting the landscaping just right, and showing off the results to friends and family. I was caught up in construction frustrations, price hikes, and delays, and while none of that is particularly enjoyable, it's part of the experience. So there I was in a beautiful new home and hadn't taken a single moment to enjoy it, to even be excited about what was being created right in front of me, and because of that, it didn't feel like home.

Other times, it's about timing. An end goal might look so far away that we don't even start the journey because the destination seems unattainable. You want to lose forty pounds, but the task of getting there feels far too imposing—it'll take a year, and I don't want it to take that long—and you don't give the goal a chance when in fact, you could lose a half pound that day. Alex Hormozi has a great tweet that reads,

> *If you can wait 90 days for a result, you can win.*
> *If you can wait a year, you can win big.*
> *If you can wait a decade, you can be the best.*
> *If you can wait a lifetime, you can change the world.*

It's important to realize you don't have to be laser focused on where you want to go and instead appreciate how you're going to get there. The dopamine boost of attaining a goal is great, but imagine having that kind of feeling *every day*. If you're gunning for a big promotion at work or you're writing the great American novel or you want to score in the big game, remember that you're creating wins every single day. Consider a traditional college student, infused with insatiable spirit and visions of great things with that degree in hand. But soon, the luster fades, and a debilitating blend of doubt and consternation sets in: Why am I doing this? I have to be here four years. What is the actual point of this class? This is costing me a fortune, and I'll be paying back loans for thirty years.

Future stressors and what-ifs cloud what is happening that day—priceless life experiences of building relationships, interacting as an adult, contributing the best of yourself, and building skills to accomplish goals. A degree is merely documentation of completing coursework; the real value of college is experiences.

If you crammed for a physics midterm and nailed it, nixed the break-room donuts, or notched ten extra reps in your daily workout, win-the-moment bracelets allow you to enjoy the day's journey and break down large goals into a smaller, more digestible size. You also appreciate the course of good decisions throughout the day instead of waiting for the end to decide if it was a good day or not. It's so much more invigorating and fulfilling being present in the midst of a journey, enjoying snippets of a great day during all of its twenty-four hours as opposed to living in a preconceived place. For example, my sister-in-law Lexe stopped over one night and was worried about a what-if scenario several years into the future. I told her it wasn't happening that day, so I wasn't worried about it. I'm not going to put any energy or thought into something that might happen three years from now, because it's not productive.

I believe we can look at daily tasks the same way. Why sink time and energy into an unknown obstacle that's not an obstacle today? The opportunity factor, of course, is no wasted time. My company experienced this while building a brand for a new client. We could see potential obstacles with their website, but we hadn't reached that part of the project yet. In strategy meetings, I'm not wasting time discussing how we'd portray X on the website if we're not to that point for another eight weeks. Instead, I focus my energy into what we're working on right now, because that's what matters, and I'll do a better job focusing on *now*.

The core of this message is so simple: stop and smell the roses. When you're on vacation, enjoy the morning sun on your face. Smile at the way your kids practice their manners at breakfast. Throw out agendas. Have a beer at 2:00 p.m. Take this same mindset to work, too, (well, maybe not the midday beer part), and keep in mind that sometimes you'll fall short of an objective, but it doesn't matter because the journey still happened, and even when you fail, good things came of it.

When I moved back to St. George after Cash was born, my plan was to start a financial practice as a financial advisor. I needed an office to get started, and it just so happened Breck was looking for an office in St. George to house a couple of his companies. It worked out perfectly, and I was able to lease one of the offices from him for my practice. What's funny is that it is still the same office I use today for my role at Vibrant Management. The creation of Vibrant came about because Breck was ready to transition his family business, the Cliffrose, into a national brand with either Hilton or Marriott, joining the Curio or Autograph collection. At this time Breck had hired me to be the CFO of the Cliffrose, so I was working with him through the transition.

It became apparent that Hilton was going to be the best fit for us and the property, and we officially started the process. During that process we realized we could no longer manage the Cliffrose unless we had a Hilton-approved management company. And everyone in the industry told us we had no chance of getting approved by Hilton: that is a huge feat. True to our fashion of making the impossible possible, we were able to get approved, and that created the launch of Vibrant Management.

When we first started Vibrant Management, I had recently moved back to St. George with plans to start a financial practice housed in the same building as Breck's company (of which I would later become CFO). When a big developer opened a new Hilton nearby, we had the opportunity to convert the Cliffrose into a Hilton four-star luxury property. In fact, Vibrant was the youngest ever of Hilton's management companies. At the time, we planned to manage only our own businesses with the hope that in the future, we could manage other people's organizations as well.

We opened our doors in April 2018 and by July, signed our first client. This was not the plan by any stretch. It was a big client: a sprawling resort near Zion National Park, spread over seven thousand acres with seventy cabins and over $5 million in annual revenue. We took on the project because the goal, of course, was to secure clients. We were very excited about it but were nowhere near ready to execute managing an organization of that size. We were ill equipped and understaffed and, in the end, fell short in a lot of places, but had we not taken on that significant challenge and failed, we wouldn't have realized the need to structure our company in a different direction. Today, we focus mainly on small boutique properties; however, in the process of fronting a great deal of money to build our brand, we realized a need for select properties, without hefty budgets, to do the same and established a brand-building segment of our team that has since worked with locations including a sprawling destination resort, Utah Luxury Tours, a Canadian fishing lodge, and even a Hawaiian skin-care line.

Ultimately, we want to be nimble to deliver what works best for us and tailor every experience to our clients' needs. It's not about maximizing net profit or X percent of gross revenue; our journey is gaining the best client opportunities balanced with quality of life. Along the way, working with so many different types of businesses, we learned to define who *we* really are—hospitality experts—and how to focus our core values to a place of where we want to be.

How to "Do" a Journey

When you make changes in your life, things will start to look different from what you're used to. If you're on a weight-loss journey and begin to feel healthier and more confident, opportunities will arise that didn't previously exist because now you are in new situations with a new lease on life. As cliché as it sounds, anything is possible when you make positive changes and work toward a goal while remaining fully present every step of the way.

The universe gives us clues and opportunities to execute life goals, but only if we tune in and listen with a willingness to take advantage of those signs. When you're focused on the journey, you don't miss things along the way. With our Disneyland road trip example, if your only focus is where you're going, it feels like it's taking much longer because it doesn't matter where you are in the moment. All you know is it's not where you want to be, so you keep looking at the clock every fifteen minutes of a four-hour drive, and you're miserable.

What if you changed that vibe? Engage in conversation with whoever else is in the car. If you're alone, queue up a podcast or get lost in your favorite music and sing like you're onstage. Go ahead and belt it out; no one can hear your off-key lyrics. Appreciate the nuances of the scenery around you. (Even the middle of Nebraska is intriguing if you give it a chance!) Do any of these things and that same drive feels completely different. An hour is an hour, but don't treat it like sixty throwaway minutes; you won't get that time back, so why not get the best of it? Time often does feel like it flies when we're having fun, in the journey. When it feels like it's dragging on forever, that's when your focus is in the wrong place: time shouldn't feel that way for us.

Another key element of an engaged journey is to ditch societal views of who you are supposed to be. I'll share a story to illustrate. I met my wife, Meagan, at a party when I was eighteen to her seventeen, and we've been together virtually every day since. At the time I was already a very driven individual, in a rush to move out of my parents' house and conquer the world. I had a beautiful townhome at age eighteen, started my first business that same year, and bought a house at twenty-one. Meagan was on a completely different wavelength, a young, impressionable girl from a small town moving to a big city without a lot of financial understanding. I became her shepherd and guide, teaching the inner workings of finances. For a time, I even charged her rent when we lived in our first house to help her learn financial responsibility. We built a life with me as her mentor, and she followed my lead. As far as she was concerned at that point, following my advice and direction was the best thing to do.

About twelve years into our relationship, she started developing new friends and discovering her individual self, with her own perspective. Part of me didn't want my wife to have her own beliefs because it was easier to just do it my way. Naturally, this drove a wedge in our relationship. She would come home and share all this "new" stuff she was learning. Thoughts and beliefs that I'd been sharing with her over the last ten years. This created a sense of frustration and hurt because she was so excited to share this newfound wisdom with me, unaware of the fact I'd been trying to share and engage in this information with her for our entire relationship. She was listening to other people and acting like they were sharing the gospel of life. What I didn't understand at the time was that she was ready to hear it for herself; it wasn't about the information that was being shared or who was sharing it. It was about her journey and the fact that she had reached the point in her life where she was ready to receive the information.

My intention is not to make light of this switch in dynamic. We didn't work through these issues over the course of a weekend; it was a very troubling, difficult time in our lives, a struggle that festered for months and inspired questions about whether the marriage would last. At the time it felt like it was on Meagan, that she was causing this strife, but upon further reflection and introspection, I realized all she was doing was growing. Change is difficult, maybe one of the biggest obstacles in life, and I was at a precipice of change, and it was up to me to decide how to handle and react to this monumental change in our dynamic.

This made me realize that in our journey, my wife was never going to be the same person that I started dating or that I married. I was certainly not the same person, and I finally recognized how wonderful it was: after a decade of Meagan walking behind me, we finally walked beside each other. Had we not experienced this difficult time together, I wouldn't have been able to appreciate and understand the value of our shared knowledge and understanding. Knowing what I know now, I wouldn't have it any other way. That's the beauty of a journey; sometimes just when you think things are taking a turn for the worse, there is a rainbow around the corner. We have a very strong and healthy marriage today, and I believe the reason why is because we were able to appreciate the journey.

Don't get lost in the past. With any long-term relationship, be open and willing to understand that they have the right to think differently tomorrow than they do today. Take political views, for example. When you married, your spouse might have been on the right, and then over time, they moved to the left. That doesn't mean that you can't have a relationship anymore; it just means your dialogue will be different, and if you're respectful of each other's opinions and beliefs, only good things come from that.

I approach new employees from that vantage as well. When I hire them, I say: "I'm hiring you to be X, but ultimately that doesn't matter because your job is whatever I ask you to do today. I may hire you to put on events, but then I may need you to go and clean a particular property. If you want to work here, I need you to understand that your job is whatever we need you to do that day, not what your title is." To that end, we don't even have titles on our business cards. I don't want to label or define something if it inspires people to feel like they don't have to do other things. Our hotels' front desk staff are not known as such. We call them guest services because if a guest has a clogged toilet or can't get the TV to work, we want that team to feel ownership of the entire guest experience, not just what happens in the lobby.

Here's another example: I've never been a religious person, but I couldn't go to a Buddha, a man who dedicated his life to his religious beliefs, and say, "Well, I'm sorry, but you're wrong." Or waltz into the Vatican and tell the pope, "I don't know what you're doing here, but you got it all wrong." That's absurd. I don't believe I have (or any of us have) enough knowledge or vindication of any one belief to say that I'm right and everybody else is wrong. For that reason, I've always considered myself a spiritual person, allowing myself to be open to any intriguing information that comes my way as opposed to being locked in to a particular set of beliefs.

Be present! And ditch preconceived notions. One of the best parts of a journey is tangible opportunities from being present and aware, but just know you'll miss them if you're already set on a particular outcome. If a neighbor invites you to a party and you grumble in advance that the party will be a dud, guess what? You've already defined the outcome, and by design, humans want to be right, and you're going into the night expecting the worst to validate your prediction, rather than enjoying the event.

This is where our subconscious comes in and drives behaviors. If you tell yourself you won't have a good time at the party or you want to lose twenty pounds and won't be happy until you do, it's a direct route to disappointment. I won't be happy until I have this, go there, do that. With that mindset, one thing is for sure—you've lost the best of the journey. Not only have you lost out on the journey, you've tabled your happiness until you arrive. What sense does that make? Why delay your happiness when you have the opportunity every day to be happy? You could have had a wonderful, fulfilling day but didn't appreciate it because you only looked to an end goal.

Is there a secret recipe to making the most of a journey and living in the moment? Some people would like me to spell it out in this book: get up at 5:00 a.m., exercise fifteen minutes to warm up, run four miles, drink muddy water from a creek, and eat only green vegetables grown in the Pacific Northwest. It's not like that. Just take the blinders off and experience life. Sound too easy? If you think it's too easy and anyone can do that, you're right. Anyone can do anything, and that's where you find your strength.

The Power of a Journey

Life journeys are incredibly powerful, and you can turn that into personal strength by tuning in to lessons along the way. So much of what we learn is gleaned through experience. Even in grade school, it's not what we learn that matters; it's that we learn to learn. What I mean by that is that school shows you how to take in new information and apply it to a task. It teaches us structure, respect, and teamwork. (And how to manage that wave of dread when you forget your locker

It's not what we learn that matters; it's that we learn to learn.

combination after Christmas break.) Navigating relationships with others, and your growing self, is school's true value, not learning 2 + 2 = 4. I remember math teachers that employed a verbal learning pep talk when asked why I needed to learn to do equations: "You're not always going to have a calculator in your pocket." This, of course, applies only to those of us born before the 1990s. Who could have imagined how wrong those teachers would be today, when not only do I have a calculator in my pocket at all times but I have a magic satellite-powered device that holds all the answers to any question in the world. Knowledge is important, but relationships show the way.

A journey is where we discover what we like and don't like, and part of turning a journey into strength is being willing to fail, setting a target so big that you don't care if you fail. In fact, I challenge you to set a target so bold and unexpected that you have only a 50 percent chance of getting there. If you fall short, it won't matter because you're still better off than not trying. But giving yourself permission to fail fuels a subconscious behavior to see a goal as an afterthought or a lesser priority. That's when you need to channel a journey's strength.

I'll share a moment that came up at work one day. As a group, we read books as a way to build camaraderie, further our knowledge, and be better humans. I realized that I had gotten everything I ever wanted in life, but I never asked for much growing up. I just didn't want to be broke; that's really what I was aiming for, and I didn't have any big, dramatic goals. I wanted to be comfortable and enjoy life and have a few nice things. I could've been wealthier and had more toys if that was a priority, but at that point, I lived in a 980-square-foot house that was safe and comfortable, and I was relatively content with the world.

But that day in the company meeting, I announced a change to my team. "You know what? I'm going to start dreaming bigger. There's no point in setting low targets all the time. I believe I can make anything happen; why am I not doing it? Living it?" I decided that day to dream bigger and two years later built my dream home, bought the two dream cars I always wanted, and wrote this book, and my company is growing exponentially.

Everything I've wanted has come true, and it's because I decided to dream bigger and stopped being afraid of falling short of any target. I literally changed nothing in my life except putting it out there that I wanted more. In fact, my day-to-day activities were worse for a while because I got into COVID-inspired bad habits and took a long time to shake them. So, while daily performance was lacking, my outcome was better because my target was bigger.

Remember that wins and failures build similar strengths. Wins build momentum and confidence to continue. Failures can create a chip on your shoulder to try harder next time and build a robust desire, or perhaps you'll realize you didn't enjoy X and won't be doing it again. I learned something I wouldn't do again at the finish line of a marathon. Since 2015 I've run at least one half marathon every year until COVID put an end to my streak in 2020. In 2016 I decided to run a full marathon, a lifelong goal and something cool to do with my dad. I ran it and missed my goal by only one minute. (Stopping to walk with my dad slowed me down, but I wouldn't trade the father-son time). It felt amazing to run the race and accomplish my goal, but I realized I much prefer half marathons and don't have any intention to run another full marathon ever again. That decision is the strength built from the journey. I realized what I do and don't enjoy, I validated that I can do anything, and I worked my ass off in training to show that when I am determined and have a target, I can make anything happen.

I know I've said not to focus on an end goal, but you still need a target to aim for. We all need a purpose in life, one that is just for us. If you have kids, friends, or a family that all need you, be there for them, but don't forget to show up for yourself too. Author and business management motivator Jim Collins encourages us to choose a BHAG, a Big Hairy Audacious Goal. Something huge that you can start working toward today and don't care if you accomplish it or not. Understand that you can't hit that goal today; it might take six months, a year, two years. The timeline is irrelevant; it's the purpose

I want you to focus on. Set that BHAG and start now. Write it down where you'll see it every day. Tell everyone what you are working toward; make your journey known. You'll create a band of cheerleaders and sometimes a few haters—people who for whatever reason don't want to see you win. Use that as motivation—show them there is a better path, and your inspiration can be theirs as well. Don't worry about reaching your big goal today; just savor the journey.

Life really is about the journey and not the destination, but you can't start a journey without a destination. The secret is not to focus on the end game. If you are simply going through the motions of life—wake up, go to work, come home, eat dinner, repeat the next day—and haven't decided where you want to go, you'll never get anywhere. When I ran my first (and only) full marathon, I wanted to finish in five hours. If it took seven hours, I wouldn't have met my goal, but I certainly didn't fail. I still completed the whole thing and crossed the finish line, and I was happy and fulfilled because I did it. Forget about what the rest of the world thinks you should be. Be present!

How to Get There

Whatever your journey, you won't arrive at its vivid, exhilarating climax today. It will take time to get there, but you can start by creating opportunities throughout every day to win the moment.

We all intuitively know how to be successful—make it happen by committing and being present every day. Want to be super fit? Dedicate a lifestyle of going to the gym five times a week, sticking to an efficient exercise regimen, eating a healthy diet. The same mindset applies to everything—landing the big job, winning a blue ribbon at the county fair, or becoming an astronaut. Just focus your energy in ways that instinctively lead you in the direction you want to go.

Your Winning Moment

It doesn't matter what your journey looks like. Maybe you want to be a better dad, lose thirty pounds, be a millionaire by age twenty, or get that corner-office promotion at work. The principles of achieving your goal are the same. If you commit to yourself, establish a Big Hairy Audacious Goal, and live intentionally, you will become the person you want to be. Remember that you don't need approval or acceptance from anyone. Manufactured views of others aren't *your* reality, nor do they validate who you are. You're in charge, and whether you're already in the midst of a journey or just starting, your next moment starts now.

Ready, Set, Goal

Now's your chance. If you have a personal or career ambition out there in front of you, record it right here. Don't wait until next week, when you're in a better mood or have more time. Don't even read the next chapter of this book. Set your goal right now.

_____

_____

_____

_____

_____

_____

_____

_____

_____

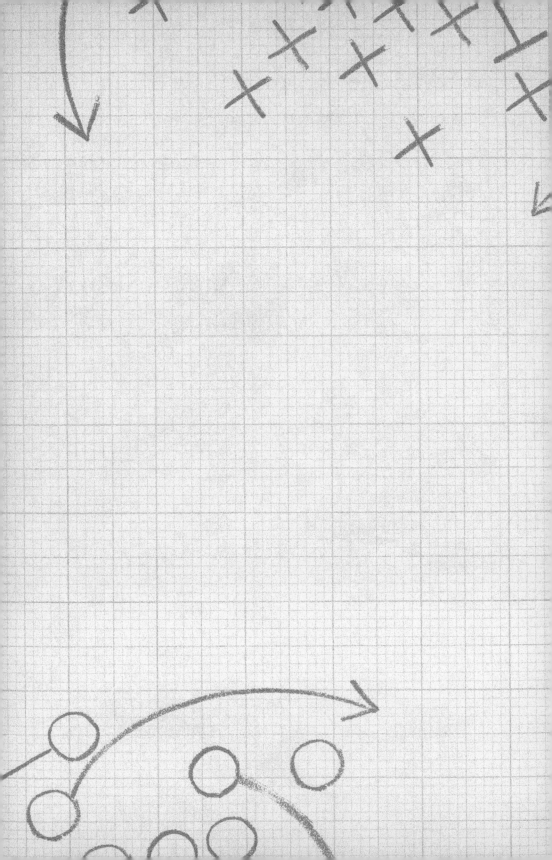

CHAPTER FIVE

CHANGE YOUR MIND, CHANGE YOUR LIFE

You cannot have a positive life and a negative mind.

—JOYCE MEYER

" I 'm such an idiot."

I know someone who utters that self-deprecating refrain every time she makes a run-of-the-mill mistake.

I keep reminding her, "You can't talk about yourself that way because then your mind goes along with it and influences a negative mindset."

Our thoughts are our most precious tools, but they can also be the most detrimental, as everything we think becomes reality. Our bodies are conditioned to do what we want them to do, and it all starts with the mind. If you say you're an idiot, your mind will find opportunities to make you believe that sure enough, you're an idiot. You wouldn't allow someone to sling derogatory names at your sister or mother or girlfriend, yet many people are willing to talk about themselves that way. What gives?

Interestingly, most of us understand the importance of physical health, eating right, and living a generally healthy lifestyle. And even if we don't do those things, we know we should. But our minds are often neglected, even forgotten, and the mind needs as much protection as the body. In fact, to me, my mind is far more important. I'd choose a paralyzed body over a compromised brain any day. As long as I have a functioning, alert mind, I can still enjoy my life with thoughts and feelings and emotion. That's what drives our lives, and that's what sparked my realization that I wasn't dreaming big enough. Like my friend the self-proclaimed "idiot," I was self-sabotaging.

Self-sabotage is as common these days as ants at a picnic. We are all guilty of it, but why do we do it? When I am in a cycle of disappointment or failure, it's easy to have that extra drink or late-night snack or sleep in and show up late for work—all things that I would never choose in a healthy state of mind. Sometimes, spiraling into that kind of cycle is about moving the starting line. Say you're going to launch a new exercise routine on April 1. Subconsciously (or maybe intentionally), you give yourself permission to have terrible habits until the first to "get it out of your system," but then April 1 rolls around, and it's a Thursday, so you decide it's better to start on Monday. Then it's a weekend of bad decisions, and Monday gets here, and it's not a great day either, and you don't feel like exercising. Just like that, you're in a loop of self-sabotage, with momentum working against you and not for you.

You can't wait until "the perfect time, when everything is just right" to fire off a life change. That time doesn't exist. The single greatest secret to results? Just start. I know that sounds too easy and hardly enlightening, but it works. If you have goals you want to reach, start today and give yourself permission to fail. None of us is perfect, but if you start your journey with that in mind, you will succeed. Don't let one misstep end all your progress. I used to stumble on that path at the beginning of a journey or life transformation. Once I'm cruising along with momentum on my side, I don't let missteps happen at all, but at the beginning, it can be easy to think it's okay to give in to temptation "just this once." But "just this once" turns into always, and pretty soon you've lost sight of your goal.

That's where your win-the-moment bracelets come into play, visual and mental guideposts that are with you all day to help you stay on track and focused. For anyone who knows me, I'm a bit of a Cookie Monster: I *love* cookies. They are my kryptonite. While in the middle of a diet program called WILDFIT, I was in the part of my journey where I wasn't allowed to have any sugar. I was at my niece Hazel's first birthday party, and they had all the good stuff—beer, chips and salsa, pizza, and of course the real killer, Crumbl Cookies! If you haven't heard of Crumbl Cookies or haven't had them yet, I suggest you google them and change that quickly. Here I was faced with my most favorite treat, piled on plates and there for the taking. It's one thing to turn down buying cookies, but when they are right in front of me, my willpower typically drops to the floor. It was at that moment that I needed a boost in willpower and a deeper purpose to say no, not to mention a dopamine hit. Thankfully, I had my win-the-moment bracelets and was able to move one of them from my left wrist to my right. The success tasted almost as good as the Crumbl Cookie would have.

It won't always be a conversation about winning; sometimes we are just choosing not to lose. When faced with an obstacle, ask yourself, "Do I want to lose?" When you take a moment to focus on what's happening, it changes the dynamic of the situation. If you are trying to cut back on soda and McDonald's offers to Super Size it for the same price, it's easy to rationalize going for the bigger one because it's a better value. But that's all it takes for the momentum wheel to come to a dead stop, shift gears, and start rolling backward on you. This is the moment you need to remind yourself, *don't choose to lose.* It's your decision. Just don't do it. And no one has power over your choices but you. McDonald's can't make you Super Size it, and you can rein in your subconscious mind's instinct to accept failure.

So much of life is autopilot, cruising through a thousand decisions every day—decisions we sometimes aren't even aware we are making. Snap out of autopilot and take control of your life with a simple statement: *don't choose to lose.* This is an illustration of the value of winning *and* losing. The allure of victory, a big job promotion, or even hitting the green light at an intersection can taint the very real benefits of coming in second. In fact, losing can propel us to great heights. We see it all the time in sports, when an athlete or team stinks up the game with a terrible loss that sticks with them, and they use that as motivation to come back stronger the next game or season. There is great power and value in being present and letting a loss be what it is: a moment in time. The key is don't let a loss live on in perpetuity and fuel the tendency to feel like a longtime loser, because that's not what you are.

For a moment, I let myself feel like I'd lost during COVID. I regained all the weight I'd worked so hard to lose in 2019, but that became my motivation to get back to healthier ways. My inspiration is the disappointment I had in myself for letting an outside influence have an effect on my body and lifestyle. It's easy to rationalize that COVID made everything more difficult and use that as an excuse, but excuses are just lies we tell ourselves. You don't need a fancy gym or even equipment to be fit and healthy. There was no reason I couldn't exercise outside and keep the healthy habits I had established, but it was easier to divert the blame from myself to the pandemic. I didn't stay focused, and that gave me the motivation to create the win-the-moment platform. Changing my mind changed my life.

The relationship with my wife is an ideal example. I had to change how I felt about her growth and realize the benefits of her transformation, and I think that too often, people are unwilling to see and accept what they can or need to change. Consider the legions of workers dissatisfied with their jobs or the political system or sky-high gas prices. It's all a matter of perspective, and while it might seem easier to be grumpy or upset, simply deciding to not let something affect you changes your relationship with it.

If you're persistently perturbed with the country's current president or doom-and-gloom newscasts bring you down, you can consciously decide not to let these things upset you. How? It starts with a choice. Don't let external factors define your day's trajectory and, ultimately, your happiness. The next time an argument festers between you and a friend, boss, or spouse, you have a choice. Fuel the fire with cutting comments that could extend the squabble for days, or … apologize and move on. No one wants to be angry, so why not just decide not to be? It sounds easy, right? In theory, it is, but the "simple" act of changing your mind can be difficult at first. You do have to dedicate some effort to recognize a scenario that needs attention and envision what it could look like in a more positive light. If your boss asks you to stay late to finish a project and you sit there fuming, you're making it worse than it is. Instead of channeling a victim mentality, stop the negative thought in midthink and realize she asked you to stay late because that's your job. Be thankful for income that helps keep a roof over your head, and realize that without a job, you wouldn't have that roof.

Sadly, with so many demands on our time and expectations for how it all should be, it's easy to become mired in a negative space and conjure images of what we think is real. If your wife leaves with friends for a girls' weekend and hasn't texted or called for a few hours, you might start imagining she's making bad choices. Pretty soon your body reacts as if she is really traipsing about with someone else—you're worried, suspicious, afraid, angry, sick to your stomach. It's like waking up from a bad dream and feeling like it's still happening. The mind can't differentiate between thoughts and reality, and we behave based on self-prescribed stories or moods. And sometimes even if reality changes the dynamic, the body's chemical makeup doesn't revert, instead holding on to the bad place, poisoning your day.

Indeed, it's tough staying positive in a world laced with perpetual bad news, unrest, manipulation, and bleak outlooks on everything from global illness to melting glaciers. Your own neighborhood might be rife with angst, pitting everyone against each other due to stories that often aren't accurate. It's okay if I think one way and you think the other, but we need to protect our minds from outside influences that constantly threaten happy, fulfilling, productive lives.

Remember that self-sabotage begins in your mind. When Friday morning rolls around and all you want to see is the weekend and you don't even want to go to work, much less put in any effort, you've preordained a shitty day. If you need to get up at 7:30 to make a morning meeting but you don't wake up until 7:50, you're instantly stressed, rushing, and your body reacts accordingly. You're still on edge at work when a coworker asks for something, and you snap at him. He thinks, Wow, what an ass, and you think it's his fault because you didn't take responsibility for *your* shit.

It's another bracelet-move moment: change your mind to accept that you overslept and inspired the day's blahs, and know that a misstep today doesn't mean tomorrow has to look the same.

Don't Step in the Muddle

I have huge respect for and take inspiration from writers like Malcolm Gladwell, Michael Lewis, and Yuval Harari. More than once, I've found myself thinking, Damn, that person is brilliant. I wish I could be like them. Funny thing is, someone might read this book and think, Wow, Cody really has it together with all these awesome antidotes. I wish I could do what he did. What they don't know (until now) is that at the core of my life remedies is a regular guy who still fails. The forty pounds I lost is back on, and I have to start over, and I'm still blaming COVID. Before that pesky virus showed up, I was killing it with two-a-day workouts on a thirty-day plan, amped for great results. Then the gym closed, I got frustrated and said, "Hell with it, the world sucks," and I stopped working out.

I need to follow my own advice! I let a misstep derail a goal, but the lesson in that for me *and* you is that awareness of your target can deflect and altogether eliminate a downward trend. Let's say one of your goals toward a healthier lifestyle is to avoid alcohol for an entire week. On the fifth day, there's a neighborhood party, and you feel you should have just one drink to be social, but it triggers something, and then you're drinking every day. That one slip gave you "permission" to step away from your goal. Not everyone reacts that way, of course, but you need to know who you are and what you're made of and understand that goals take different forms.

If I missed one day going to the gym but never claimed that as a target, it's not a big deal to just go the next day. But if I say I'm going every day and miss one, a bad seed can germinate to foster another missed day or "I might as well wait until Monday" or other reasons to put it off. If it's October and your New Year's resolution is to be healthier, why on earth are you waiting ninety days? Why not be healthy *on* New Year's Day? We allow one-off fails to ruin everything because we're focused on the destination, and then we often go on to feel like a global failure.

But part of the power of winning the moment is giving ourselves permission to fail, because we're all going to fail sometime. Humans are prone to allow failure to multiply, but here's the scoop: Success and failure work the same way. Momentum works in whatever direction you're headed, and good momentum equals positive results. When you're faced with bad momentum, it's hard to stop. I moved a meeting last week, and it was easy, so I moved another one. That's not how you become successful. There has to be some structure for success in whatever fashion you're going for. Moving that one meeting indirectly gave me permission to move others, and with snowballing bad momentum, it would be easy to let delays mount and keep canceling meetings. Excitement and focus dwindle, and next thing you know, two months pass, and the project is doomed. Now you're in a state of panic, rushing to finish, and quality inevitably suffers.

Simply preparing foundation tasks can feel overwhelming, even though the actual task of the thing is the same. One member of my team has a procrastination tendency that came to a head when we switched operating systems, his quarterly goal, at one of our properties. Conversion was scheduled on site Monday and Tuesday—he had a panic attack on Sunday. He'd been working on the project for six months but waited until the last minute, essentially making something that wasn't difficult into an absolutely terrifying moment. It's not that the task was overwhelming; his approach made it feel that way.

Here's another example of how one misstep can turn a manageable hill into a mountain. I skipped going to the gym so long that self-made stories became manufactured realities. I kept telling myself, When I finally go back, staff will ask where I've been and take one look at me and wonder, What the hell happened? He put a bunch of weight back on. And other members will watch me hyperventilate on the treadmill or attempt rudimentary jumping jacks and make fun of me. I told myself all these terrible stories, and now my body believes them and tenses up at even the thought of going back to the gym.

That's where thoughts creep in of classifying yourself as a failure, and this is *the* big moment when you need to remember you are not a failure; your behaviors and activities were. Step back and understand we are not preconditioned to fail. If you behaved in a way indicative of failure, know that it's not you as a person, and remove failure's power. Rip it right out of its clingy grasp. One highly effective way to do that is owning your shit. It can be difficult for some people to step up and take responsibility for their actions, but it is incredibly powerful, and once you get in the habit, it becomes a lifelong remedy for all that ails you.

I was thrust into a situation just like this during my district manager tenure at Wireless Advocates. Every region had weekly conference calls with the leadership team, and at the time, I was training a new DM. As a whole, we'd had a rough sales weekend, and our regional manager was addressing each district in alphabetical order, becoming increasingly peeved with every letter.

Each manager droned on for ten or fifteen minutes, making excuses for their teams' dismal performances. Steve's LA team had floundered because he has personal stuff going on. Mike in Colorado can't seem to maintain sales numbers. Ruben's team sees more customer complaints than sales. This pattern continued, and no one took responsibility. At this point Sharon was ready to boil over, going after my peers for everything they said with a tongue-lashing breakdown of their weekend performance, until she arrived at my district.

The manager finally got to me, sufficiently exasperated by then, and said, "Well, what about you, Cody? What happened in your district?"

I replied with comfortable confidence, "You know what, Sharon? I wasn't a very good leader this weekend. I wasn't very present with my team, and I didn't motivate them in the way that I'm capable of. I didn't have productive communication, and that's on me, and I'm going to do better going forward."

"Okay, sounds great."

I talked for thirty seconds, and she moved on. My DM trainee looked at me in disbelief and asked what the hell had just happened.

"She doesn't need to go after me because I took responsibility," I said. It was a brief but potent lesson of owning failure for what it is and leveraging it to win the moment. We are all reflections of our experiences, with the capability to harness emotions and actions that reflect who we are.

The Power of Winning and Losing

Winning is exhilarating. You might have just won the Boston Marathon or summited Denali or finished your college dissertation.

Losing doesn't come with the same endorphin boost, but it is no less powerful. Think way, way back to the earliest pyramid-building Egyptians, among mankind's most brilliant minds, who nevertheless faced defeat. In fact, much of our history as a human race was built on empires that won and lost. But we remember the victories, not the losses. Even Sunday-afternoon football battles hold similar influence. Unless the losing team in the last Super Bowl is your favorite team, we remember who won the game, not the runner-up. After your final day here on earth, the eulogy will be made of stories of your wins, not the times you blew it.

This is an unfortunate injustice in life's win-loss theater. We endure losses nearly every day, from childhood to golden years, but we overlook how moments and stories of wins of all shapes and sizes are often fueled by losing. Personally, much of who and what I am today was shaped by my struggles. In chapter two I mentioned how my learning obstacle made me feel lesser than other kids and stupid. Now that experience drives an insatiable thirst for knowledge and motivation to become an expert in my field. It also helps me be a better father to my daughter, who is experiencing the same struggles that I did at her age. I wouldn't be the kind of father or industry professional I want to be without my childhood losses and lessons.

When people reminisce about life's ups and downs, they inevitably say, "I wouldn't change a thing," that time-tested adage fueled by hindsight, stubborn pride, and sometimes, veiled regret. When I was in my twenties and lost every penny I had and then some, I didn't think it was such a wonderful time, but it was an Oscar Wilde moment: youth is wasted on the young. I didn't have the wisdom to see the bigger picture and hadn't yet built a belief that I would pull myself out of that difficult place, but looking back, I'm grateful for the experience because the losses helped inspire my drive for a brighter future and taught me to listen to my gut and be more cautious with my investments.

When we are young, it's impossible to see the bigger picture, but nothing is the same forever. The only constant is change. That's how we build strength from losses; it's a lesson learned of what *not* to do, and sometimes that holds more value than knowing, or thinking you know, what to do. We fall faster than we can get up, like an instantaneous stock market plummet to zero that never skyrockets at that same speed. Realizing as much can save your hide in challenging times and, best of all, provides teachable moments that stay with you for life.

Consider winning at its most fundamental parts. It doesn't take much wisdom or effort to explain the strengths of winning. We learn how fun it is at a young age, and the joy of it sticks with us, like learning to ride a bike. I don't have to worry about teaching my kids the will to win; it's instinctual. At ages five and eight, Cash and Olivia already race to see who can put their shoes on first or be the first to the mailbox or to sprint upstairs to brush their teeth. They are always looking for ways to win.

Where does that spirit go when we grow up? I certainly don't see that kind of vigor in any of the adults I know, and I believe that is because without a healthy relationship with winning *and* losing, it's easy to stop trying to win. You can't lose if you don't even try to win, a concerning epidemic in today's world. Remember that competing is healthy and fun but losing is a learned skill. My kids love racing up the stairs or across the backyard, but whoever loses has a complete breakdown. Even with nothing but pride and determination on the line, losing still has a devastating impact.

While writing this chapter, I realized life is so much more than winning the moment. How many books talk about losing, and who wants to read about that anyway? I know how to win moments, but I never learned how to lose and develop a positive relationship with it. But one of life's most important balances is being aware that there are always opposite sides to everything—good and bad, fun and boring, fast and slow, happy and sad. Losing would be a hard pill to swallow if we never, ever won, right? We all need to feel the jubilation of a win, and that's largely what this book is all about. Even if I'm just playing in our family's World Foosball Championship—dad and son against wife and daughter—the victory still feels so good.

I love to win! And anyone who knows me knows that too. The beauty of winning the moment is learning to recognize opportunities to win throughout the day, and the best part is it's not about society's definition of winning and losing: no one else dictates if you win or lose; *you* decide what it looks like, with the power to control how you play the game.

To fully illustrate the power of winning the moment, we must create an understanding of momentum. Life's most valuable asset is time, and time builds on itself like compound interest. Picture yourself cruising across Interstate 15, smack in the middle of Utah, and you pass a vintage Cadillac Eldorado with whitewalls and fuzzy dice hanging from the rearview mirror. Up the road a piece, you make a quick five-minute rest stop, then hightail it back on the highway, and before long, you're passing the same Caddy you passed a half hour ago. That's an example of compound interest: the simple fact that the Cadillac never stopped allowed it to make up thirty minutes on you even though you only stopped for five minutes.

This is also an illustration of momentum. When we accomplish our goals repeatedly, day after day after week after month, without a pit stop, we can accomplish truly incredible things. Once you get that sweet taste of victory, you are more motivated to taste it again. If you win the day and move all ten bracelets, your drive to do it again the next day increases exponentially. We see this in sports all the time. I'm a basketball nut and remember when the Golden State Warriors got on a roll in 2015 and it seemed like it would never end. Then came a slew of injuries and Kevin Durant's departure and missing the playoffs. They turned it around in 2022, winning another NBA championship. Once they lost momentum, it took four years to get it back. How many of us had similar obstacles? Did COVID derail your momentum? Some other obstacle? Whatever life's challenges, you can harness the power of momentum and start winning the moment today!

I'd like to share the powerful example of change your mind, change your life with Don Miguel Ruiz's *The Four Agreements*. One of his rules is Don't Make Assumptions. Its simplicity is as powerful as its purpose. How often have you received an email or text message and made an assumption about the sender's tone that shapes your mood for the rest of the day? I know I've responded to messages with more vitriol than was necessary as I made assumptions on the sender's behalf. Ruiz elaborates on this with views on assuming positive intent. Giving the sender the benefit of the doubt changes everything and was a powerful message for me. It's incredible how we can put so much value on words. I've received emails from people I didn't gel with in the past, and without assuming positive intent, the emails seemed unprofessional, uncalled for, and even downright rude. But when I read them and assumed positive intent, I saw they were honest efforts to have a better understanding of a complicated subject.

We are the reality we create.

In that moment of reading an email that made my skin boil, all I had to do was change my mind, and everything else changed along with it. I can be a little feisty when challenged and in this case thought only of myself and fired back a crude and hard email, only to regret it shortly thereafter. I hadn't yet learned the power of my thoughts and my mind.

Remember that we are the reality we create. A place filled with opportunities and positivity starts in our minds, and a changed mind brings a changed life.

Mind over Matter

My younger sister Sarah always lived in a what-if world, stressed about the future. She's done great in life so far, but doom and gloom weighed on her—what if I run out of money, what if that doesn't work, what if I don't like the new job? She literally worried herself sick, and I finally told her, "Sarah, you can't live in the future. None of those thoughts are productive, and you can't make your future life work today. You can't do it until you get there." Her story drives home the importance of changing the way you think about things and only focusing on what you can control in the moment. You can't do it until you get there, and in the meantime, direct your mind toward winning moments and recognize there is power in losing as well.

How to Get There

It's important to understand that you can't lose twenty pounds in a day. You can't get the big job promotion in one day, hit your savings goals, or beat your personal record in the local 5K. It takes time and is something you actively need to work toward. But most of us understand when we do something counterproductive to an initiative. It's not productive if you're trying to lose weight and go to Dairy Queen twice a week. But we also know what it feels like to win in the moment. If you can't sleep because you're worried about a meeting in two weeks, tell your mind to knock it off. Don't get crabby because you can't lift as much weight as you'd like on the first day of training. Your brain needs exercise just like every other muscle in your body, and you can use it to shape your life the way you want it to be.

Your Winning Moment

It sounds so easy, but it works. Your mind is extraordinarily powerful, and leveraging that strength can alter your life's direction, appearance, feel, and fulfillment. The most dramatic, and fastest, way to transforming your life is by controlling your thoughts. It doesn't matter if it's exercise, career, or delicate situations with coworkers, friends, or loved ones. How many times have you dreaded a future conversation and then it turned out to be painless? Your mind made the moment worse than it was and put your body through loads of stress. Be honest with where you're at and what you're thinking, and do what works for *you*. Your life will follow that lead and reward you in wonderful ways.

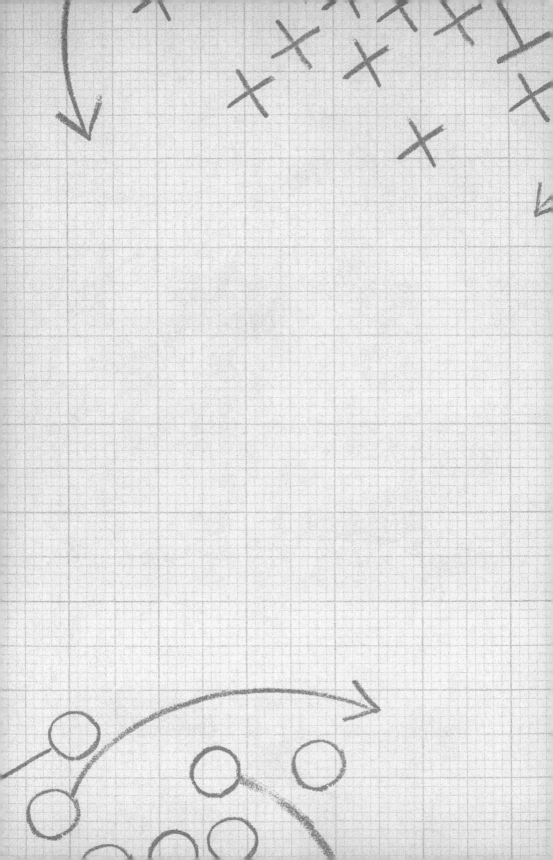

CHAPTER SIX

LET THE UNIVERSE BE YOUR GUIDE

*And, when you want something, all the universe
conspires in helping you achieve it.*

—PAULO COELHO, *THE ALCHEMIST*

L ife is like a forever-flowing river, and the universe will forge a path that leads to wherever you want to go. But there's a catch. You can't just sit back and wait for wonderful things to happen. The universe needs to know you're there. If you remain stagnant as a London palace guard, the path ahead will be undefined and confusing, leaving you mired at a directionless crossroads. But you get to decide; you are in ultimate control of your destiny. If you're truly committed, the universe will provide opportunities and clear the way ahead.

That's how this book came together. As I sized up a tenth fairway sand trap playing golf on a sunny Sunday afternoon, Breck said I should write a book. I'll blame his random disruption for my shank into the sand, but the next day, an email showed up with an invitation from a publisher. A week later, I attended a work conference in Ogden, Utah, and that evening joined a few colleagues for downtime at a local bar. On the way out, we noticed a handful of homeless people milling about. One had greeted me as we arrived, and my thirst for meeting people and understanding what they're about inspired a spontaneous conversation. I sat down on the curb with him, and he introduced himself as Hobo Jesus, with a fascinating backstory and skills like reading palms. He offered to read mine, and one of the premonitions gave me goosebumps. "You're supposed to write a book. You're working on making it happen but haven't done it yet." Coincidence? Malarkey fortune-telling? Perhaps, but I saw and welcomed both events as unexpected signs. I felt a pull that this was something I should listen to, like the life opportunity I had after being booted from my first business venture. I could've pissed and moaned about losing a great job or turned a cup-half-full outlook into something better. This was a similar scenario. Writing a book would certainly not be easy; I still had to make it work financially, dedicate the time commitment, and learn what it takes to get my name on the cover. But the universe provided an occasion that hadn't been there when I woke up that day, and I accepted it.

Here we are in chapter six, author and reader, onward as partners in a great big life adventure, an exhilarating example that if you're willing to put in the work and be clear and conscious about what you want, life's road will open wide.

It reminds me of being a kid and telling Santa what you want for Christmas, speaking to a mythical being you're wishing into existence in hopes that somehow a new toy shows up under the tree. That's how the universe works—you have to keep professing your desires. As little tykes, we tend to expect to get up the next morning, race downstairs to the tree, and have a pile of loot under there. As adults, it's important not to lose sight of what's realistic but never stop dreaming. Think of it like this:

Maintain positive intent, look for signs, create opportunities. Interestingly, we often see the signs and think, I should do this, but fear or uncertainty stops us in our tracks. That sends the universe a signal that you're not ready or don't really want it. My sister fell into this pattern after the initial COVID wave in 2020. She was one of the legions of Americans who made more money through stimulus checks and unemployment than she did at her job. Her temporary savings "nest egg" ballooned to an impressive size for her, but in an eyeblink it was gone, and she lamented, "I wish I never got that money in the first place."

"Are you listening to yourself?" I said. "You need to fix your relationship with money right now. You have a poor relationship with money, but you still desire it and want more of it. The universe gave you a bunch of cash, and now you wish you never got it in the first place. Because of that conversation, the universe now sees that Sarah doesn't like free money because she doesn't appreciate it. You should look at it as the best thing that could've happened at the time." I pointed out the lesson of what not to do with extra money and how to leverage that knowledge into becoming more financially educated. More importantly, she learned her words and actions spurred her subconscious to create a negative state.

Life can be a tough road, and it can be difficult to channel an always-positive mindset, but it's less about thinking positive and more about being clear. Don't just say you want a nice car; be precise. "I want a white Corvette with a black interior and red stitching." Be clear with your intentions about what you want and when and how you want it to be. That's how it all comes together.

Sarah continued, "I want to be financially free."

"What does that mean to you?"

"I don't know."

I laughed and said, "Well, how the hell are you going to get there? You want to be financially free, but you don't even know what it looks like. You heard somebody else say that, and it sounded good, but it's their goal, not yours. You never told yourself what 'financially free' means. You've created an aspiration that's impossible to achieve because you never defined what that means for you. This is going to leave you feeling like a failure because you never hit your goal, because your goal was an undefined illusion you could never reach."

She needed to be clear with her intentions and what was important to help bring them to life. In the end, arriving at a place you've always wanted gives it exponential value.

A friend of mine had a life goal of working in the conservation arena for National Geographic. He was committed to that dream and, after a litany of rejections, recently landed a spot on the team. I believe declaring his intention made it happen. Keep in mind if something along the way derails a dream, don't let failure deter you. My friend heard a "no" the first few times but didn't give up and recalibrate his goals to something else. He wasn't afraid of rejection, instead turning it into a new opportunity that played even closer to his strengths. His desire to be in that place didn't change, and the universe found a way to make it a life-changing reality.

Did something magical happen? Was an otherworldly force at work to get him that job? Nope, it was life in action. Actor Will Smith, another believer in the universe, says, "There's a redemptive power that making a choice has rather than feeling like you're an effect to all the things that are happening. Make a choice. Just decide what it's gonna be, who you're gonna be, how you are going to do it.

Just decide. And from that point, the universe will get out of your way."[5] He's right. Don't make it more complex than it needs to be, and don't be afraid of failure. When people ask if I'm spiritual or what I believe, I say I believe in the universe. It's not just a goal-oriented thing for me; it's a lifestyle, similar to a religious view of right from wrong and being happy for other people. I'm genuinely happy for my friend's success, and I believe the universe sees that as a positive and wants to propel goodness forward, living life as intended.

Here's a Christmas-holiday example. My friend Andrew's law firm has a tradition of giving money to families in need in our community. They choose four families and spread $1,000 among them; not a large monetary donation, but generous all the same, especially during the holidays. This past year, Andrew asked if other local businesses wanted to join the cause, and we banded together to give away $6,000 to twenty-four families. We had to select the families most in need, and it was heart wrenching, reading their stories; I wanted to give to all of them and wouldn't settle for average. The group sent a message to the other businesses that it wasn't enough, and we recruited more to boost our donation to fifty-one families! Next year we set the goal to give away $100,000.

It can seem like it takes forever or maybe will never happen, but doing good things really does come back to you. Good takes time, but when so much of our lives today pulse with instant gratification, many people stumble because they don't want to wait. It's not enough to whiz through a McDonald's drive-through; now you can have a Big Mac delivered to your door and harden your arteries without delay.

---

5   Will Smith, "Will Smith Power of Choice - *The Alchemist*," video, 00:40, https://www.youtube. com/watch?v=EnUS1XFasWc.

The right-now world is fine in some respects, but don't ever forget that life has a finite clock and that last tick of the hands comes way too fast. A teenager sees his years ahead as having no end, while a recent retiree recognizes her golden years for what they are. Regardless of your place in life, good things come if you follow the universe's lead. If you're, say, a plumber but want to be something else, you need to change what you're doing and capitalize on new opportunities, or you'll be a plumber forever. Nothing wrong with that if it's your calling. If you hear a different ring, however, answer it!

I lived a similar scenario when I ran my marketing company in Houston. I was very successful, managing a solid contract with multiple professional sports teams, and then Meagan got pregnant with our second child. I knew I'd be leaving the company and moving back to Utah to raise our family but didn't know for sure what I would do next. St. George is an incredible place to live and work, but it's still growing and doesn't have enough companies with high-paying positions to support a family. I wouldn't have had to leave for Phoenix and Houston if it did. That created a lot of uncertainty with the move back home. I was starting a practice as a financial advisor, something I'm truly passionate about, but it didn't come with any level of security. I was six months into building my practice when my business partner, Breck, presented a new opportunity with a steady income to balance my commission-only business. I felt the universe pull toward another life chapter and dove in. It turned out to be a very lucrative decision, but had I not been willing to recognize the chance and do the work, it wouldn't have happened.

How many people do you know who, when in need of a job and offered one, turn away because "it's not for me"? It doesn't pay enough; it's too far away; I don't want to do that kind of work. They're missing the bigger picture. It's not just what the job will do for you but rather the opportunity cost of what could come from that job. I wouldn't have anything I have in life today if I hadn't taken the opportunity to earn it. It's easy to look back with "I should've done it when I had the chance" vision, but life doesn't work like that. You never know what can happen, and recognizing opportunities circles back to momentum and winning the moment.

The Winner Effect

Thomas Jefferson said, "If you want something you've never had, you must be willing to do something you've never done."[6] I didn't know it before writing this book, but there is a biological element to that statement, and it drives my core belief about winning. Piles of research from renowned experts around the world call it "the winner effect," a long-term shift in a person's brain structure that boosts confidence and sharpens the ability to face and conquer significant challenges. Winning literally changes our biology, giving our brains a big hit of testosterone and dopamine that shapes our behaviors, and this phenomenon takes place on stages from Wall Street to grade school spelling bees to the Super Bowl. Ian Robertson, cognitive neuroscientist at the University of Cambridge, sums up his research in one succinct declaration: "Winning increases the dopamine receptors in the brain, which makes you smarter and more bold."[7]

I've channeled the winner effect since those days of hawking snacks from my parents' pantry, becoming decidedly bolder with every new challenge. Subsequent years dialed in my trust in the universe, and I believe the two work together in a big ole snowball

---

6   "If you want something you have never had (Spurious Quotation)," Monticello, Accessed September 21, 2022, https://www.monticello.org/research-education/thomas-jefferson-encyclopedia/if-you-want-something-you-have-never-had- spurious-quotation/.

7   Ian Robertson, *The Winner Effect* (New York: Bloomsbury, 2013).

effect that establishes a win today and makes us more aware of the next exhilarating opportunity.

I saw this happen one day with Breck in our office. He started the day renewing a couple of clients, closed another related business deal, and nailed a big meeting with a high-profile property owner in town. By 4:00 p.m. that day he had a string of wins, each building on the sense of accomplishment gained from the first one. The same evolution happens if you're kicking the giant-soda habit. At first you didn't think you could stop guzzling huge quantities of soda, but then you did, creating a new sense of belief in yourself that goes on to win the next milestone. Closing a million-dollar business deal and walking away from a Big Gulp are obviously different challenges, but the winner effect is alive in both, changing the mind's biochemistry and increasing your confidence.

What's happening is building a foundation for wins, with small habit changes. Marathon runners don't go out and run twenty-six miles the first day, right? A "little" win to start sets the mood, and once it takes hold, we tend to return for more. If you make the first jump against your buddy in checkers, most people believe they will go on to win the game. A stock trader who notches three solid trades and a huge return is more likely to keep trading.

Just like mice. Studying the winner effect, scientists plunked two mice into a miniature gladiator ring and let them go at it. Nearly every time, the winner of the first match went on to win the next one and the one after that, returning every time to the place where they won. Losing mice, on the other hand, avoided that place.[8] I felt like a losing mouse during my weight-loss journey when the gym became a detractor rather than inspiration. I avoided going back because I

---

8   Ian Robertson, *The Winner Effect* (New York: Bloomsbury, 2013).

didn't want to lose, but in the end I took away the chance to win again. And I didn't get the cheese!

Remember that it's not about amassing ten huge milestones at once; a surplus of small wins steadily builds confidence. If I hit the golf course after a long winter and triple-bogey the first hole, I'm in a mental funk and the entire round generally sucks, but if I birdie that hole, I feel like I'm set for a course record. My skills don't evaporate over the winter, but my mental capacity sometimes does; I just need to be aware of that and adjust on the next hole. It took me a long time to harness this skill; one bad hole used to ruin my entire round. On more than one occasion, Breck has doubled over in laughter at the sheer joy of watching one of my mental meltdowns on the golf course. I'll never forget my round at Wolf Creek, a famous course in Mesquite, Nevada. I started off terribly and shanked multiple balls in a row. This brought great joy to Breck, as I am usually able to keep my cool, but not on this day. I let the slow start ruin my entire round at a course I was so excited to play. Thankfully, I've finally built my mental muscles to the place I can have a triple bogey but stay focused and keep my confidence I will still win the round. The same thing can happen at work. If your boss thinks the project you just turned in is garbage, it shatters your confidence going forward. That's when you need to recognize that one loss does not drive the script. Your life's next scene, whether it's an hour from now or tomorrow or next month, is another opportunity to win.

For me, the high of winning took hold very early, like on the soccer field at age seven, when I was a terrible-to-average player but my team was great and we won every game. It gave me confidence to do anything, anywhere, and that drive hasn't abated as an adult. Even board games with my kids turn competitive because I want them to learn the value of earning a victory. (And I not-so-secretly love being our family's Guess Who? world champ.) Keep in mind, however, that too much bravado can backfire. I've seen people succeed and fail my whole life, and it's easy to spot the difference. We all have a relative, friend, or coworker who perpetually fails and throws the blame elsewhere—my boss was a jerk, the company is stupid, the other guy made me look bad.

I remember some members of my team at Wireless Advocates followed this trajectory at times when they didn't have a good sales day. They grumbled that only a few customers came into the store or our deals weren't good enough—anything that was outside of their control. I tried to redirect their "loss" into a more driven, positive mindset: How many new sales calls did you make? If customers didn't say yes, how did you direct the conversation? Did you create value when asking for the sale? Instead of finding a peripheral reason for a bad day, I wanted them to find something they could do better tomorrow, because if you can't own your actions, a negative feedback loop pulls you into its clutches, and escape can be a long time coming.

The same thing happened in my cellular sales district in Utah with Verizon. At the time, the focus was on selling tablets, but demand for them wasn't exactly red hot. That, of course, inspired common gripes from staff about their low sales numbers because "no one wants tablets." In those days, entire districts would maybe sell two to three tablets in a day, and I was tired of my team's gloomy outlook. I sent an email one morning with my plans to go to X location and sell five tablets that day. I accomplished it, and almost immediately, the usual excuse mongering started: "You might have done it at Providence, but no way you could do that in Hurricane." The next day I showed up in Hurricane and did it there too. After that I asked the district teams which store I should go to next. All told, I sold five tablets at every store in the district over a seven-day stretch in a real-time demonstration to my team that anything is possible if you want it and eliminate excuses to get there. I'll admit I was a tad nervous to start, but once I nailed that first store, I knew I could keep doing it. I had a goal, vocalized it, and arrived at the destination.

But what about obstacles? Life certainly isn't a proverbial walk in the park, and while the universe provides opportunity, it also presents challenge. It's up to you to decide how to manage it. Say you're on a road trip to wherever and get a flat tire. You won't let it derail your vacation; you'll pull over and fix that thing straight away. An obstacle doesn't mean the journey is over; it just looks different, and you might need to pivot in a new direction that either still leads to your destination or presents an entirely new one. Keep in mind you will almost always encounter pitfalls, frustration, and interim failure, but knowing things can get wobbly gives you the ability to stabilize them.

When you have a real goal worth achieving and one that will change your life, nothing should stop you from reaching it. If small obstacles get in the way, then your goal isn't big enough or you're not committed to it. At Vibrant, we experienced more than one hanging-by-a-thread moment, like that time I needed a client's invoice paid or I wouldn't make payroll, or when COVID caused all our clients to let us go, and we had $11.37 left in our company account.

When it's down to the wire, or even if you're just a little unsure, envision your destination and know you want it, and you'll do what it takes to make it happen.

Guiding to Wins

The universe won't decide your destination for you; you're in control. But if you want the universe to be a guide to your journey, you have to let it know where you are going. I believe this works in any aspect of life, whether it's a job you want, a car, or a certain amount of funds in your savings. What matters most is that you are crystal clear in your desire for that thing. It can't be a dip-your-toes-in-the-water moment; you must be fully committed because you will hit roadblocks and obstacles along the way. The universe will support you, but it will also test you at times. Keep your destination in view, and *go*.

How to Get There

Be present. Sound too easy? Sometimes we think life is more complex than it really is, but none of the principles shared in this book take a special or uniquely gifted person to execute. In fact, they are relatively easy. Paulo Coelho states this perfectly in *The Alchemist*: "There is only one thing that makes a dream impossible to achieve: the fear of failure."[9] It takes awareness of your surroundings and an ability to recognize them for what they are, but you *can* do it. Not all signs are created equal. Sometimes a sign from the universe will be as clear as a freeway billboard; other times it might be a whisper in the wind. In either case, you have to present enough to notice in order to capitalize on and take advantage of opportunities. And remember that missing a sign is not the same as quitting. You just have to find an alternate route. Keep your daily activities aligned with your target destination or goal, and the universe will give you the support you need.

---

9   Paulo Coelho, *The Alchemist* (New York: HarperCollins, 1993).

Your Winning Moment

No one ever achieved great success on their own. You've got to have help from somewhere, and I don't think anything is more powerful than the universe. Get to know it, trust in it, and the next time an obstacle appears, you have a stalwart, inspiring partner to help you turn challenge into possibility. With a head of steam like that, nothing can stop you. The universe is easy to work with, and it wants you to succeed; you just have to be willing to put in the work. It's that easy.

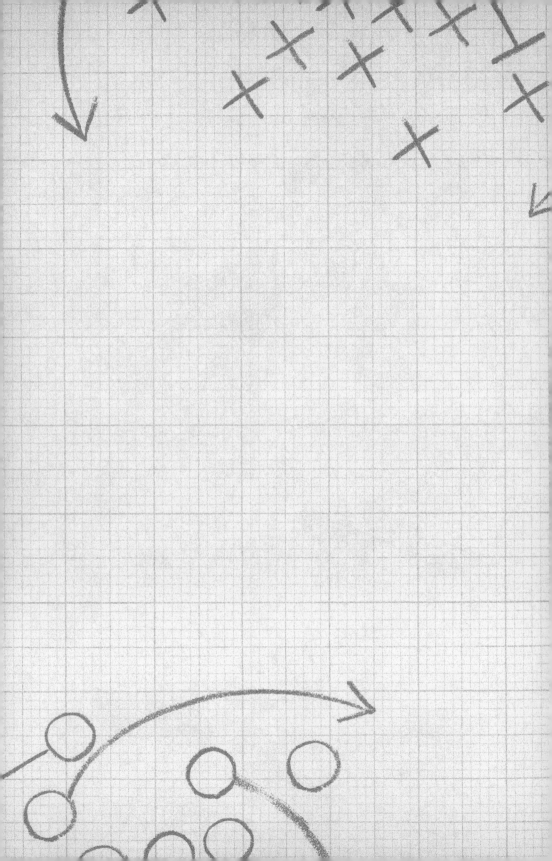

CHAPTER SEVEN

OBSTACLES ARE OPPORTUNITY

You may encounter many defeats, but you must not be defeated. In fact, it may be necessary to encounter the defeated, so you can know who you are, what you can rise from, how you can still come out of it.

—MAYA ANGELOU

O bstacles always get a bad rap. It's easy to blame them for all that ails us, but they aren't the devil incarnate. In fact, with a blend of perspective and hindsight, obstacles don't have to become a negative drain on your life. Think back to a time when something devastating, or even temporarily annoying, happened to you. In the moment, you probably didn't think it was great that you lost your job or hit all the red lights on the way to an important meeting or went down for a month with COVID. That's because you didn't have the ability to understand what it all meant for your future, that there was a better opportunity down the road. No one has a crystal ball (that works), but if you could see the future, that earlier obstacle wouldn't have ruined your day.

We live in a world of duality, with joy and happiness paralleling contradicting struggle, but struggle is what makes success feel so exhilarating. If every day was perfect, it would no longer feel perfect. It would feel average, and I don't know anyone who wants an average life. We don't want to ride a roller coaster around a flat circle, right? The ups and downs are what makes it fun.

Life really is like a roller coaster. You can't fully appreciate the purpose of difficult times without understanding the value of obstacles. When I lost every penny I had, I was an emotional and physical wreck. Every day was glum, and every night all I wanted to do was watch *Rob & Big* on MTV to distract me from my failure. At that time of my life, I hadn't yet learned to flex my mental muscles and wasn't equipped with the knowledge I have today. Even worse, I was too ashamed to talk to anyone about my struggles and just let them fester and ruin every aspect of my day and my closest relationships. I had to put in a lot of work to get myself out of that funk and see there was light past the darkness. In the thick of it, I would have given anything to not experience that pain, but now I look back on it as one of the most important lessons in my life, if not the best. I wouldn't change it for the world. In fact, I went through *two* periods when I could afford to eat only one meal a day, usually a ninety-nine cent Totino's pizza or, if I was feeling fancy, Hamburger Helper. (Cheeseburger Macaroni was my favorite.)

> *You can't fully appreciate the purpose of difficult times without understanding the value of obstacles.*

Those challenging times taught me that I can get through anything and gave me the confidence to remove my fear of failure. I've stumbled and failed plenty of times but always got back up and was stronger because of it. Every failure created mental scar tissue that inspired the ability to take risks because if I lose everything again, I know I will get it back. My dad endured a similar situation and one familiar to millions of people around the world when he and my mom divorced. She left him, and it destroyed his mental and behavioral state for several years. He couldn't pay the mortgage for a while, got behind on car payments, and spiraled into a perpetual negative space. Eventually, he sold the house and, through the sale, unemployment, COVID stimulus checks, and other aligning stars, he's now in the best financial situation of his life with a new partner and beautiful home, living a happy retired life. At the time of the divorce, he would have done whatever he could to change that, but today, he couldn't imagine it not happening.

Although heartbroken and distressed in our respective situations, neither of us could duplicate the lessons without the losses. What are some obstacles or failures you have endured, and what came next? I'm sure every one of you can connect the dots from those difficult times to a positive future. Certainly, not everything is positive, but it's important to understand that it's okay to be upset and frustrated and disgusted with obstacles. Just remember that it's not forever. We have to experience the difficult things in life and be present enough to feel that pain, but that pain is temporary and can be a catalyst for positive outcomes ahead.

We also tend to overanalyze thoughts on failure and let them chafe like bad underwear. When we win, we typically don't sit down and really think about what made that possible; we celebrate and move on to the next opportunity. Not a lot of learning takes place. Devastating losses, however, stick with us and cultivate extended periods of mulling over "could have, should have" regrets. As uncomfortable as it often is, this is when the most growth takes place. Let's say you go to the gym to channel your best Schwarzenegger and lift the same weight every day. Your muscles will never grow, and you won't get any stronger. The only way to build more muscle and strength is to push past your comfort level and challenge yourself to improve.

You should pursue the same habits in everyday life. Call it intentional discomfort, and know that's when real growth happens. If you're comfortable the entire day at work, you didn't stretch your talents enough. Did you miss an opportunity to showcase an idea or challenge a process you know isn't working? Do you hesitate to broach a sensitive topic at family gatherings because it's "easier" to leave it alone? Don't run away from uncomfortable; embrace it. You're getting stronger every day.

One of my big growth moments happened on the driveway at my childhood home in Cheyenne, Wyoming. I practiced shooting hoops nearly every day, but with most any sport, you can improve only so much doing it on your own, so I always asked my dad to play. He never let me win and had a way of nurturing my skills while shaping an appreciation for earning victory. That moment came on a cold winter evening, hardly favorable conditions for outdoor basketball, but the temperature didn't faze us—we were heated from an intense "home court" battle. I was eight or nine years old at the time and growing taller, with a bit more reach and agility. Dad executed a perfect jab step and then faded away for a midrange jumper, but I timed it perfectly and swatted the ball away like a pesky insect. If TikTok had existed back then, the scene would have gone viral; instead, it was just the two of us (mostly me) to enjoy the moment, and we laughed at what was happening. It was game point, and I had the ball, drove to the right, pump faked, and did the scoop move he showed me, dropping the ball right through the net. I sprinted into the house to tell Mom I had finally done it. *"I beat Dad!!"* Losses prior to that night made the victory so sweet for me. Along with the win, I learned the unfettered jubilation of overcoming an obstacle.

Obstacles and You

I want to help you change your relationship with obstacles. Like we discussed with winning and money, it's about why. Why should you adjust your view of and relationship with obstacles? To me, it boils down to controlling your thoughts. Left to its own devices, your mind can make a run-of-the-mill obstacle feel far worse than it is, and before you know it, you're imagining terrible, stressful things that aren't even happening. Instead, try this: "I don't know why this happened, but I know it will have a benefit for me in the future and I won't be in this tough place forever."

I don't know anyone whose life is what they thought it would be, including me. I certainly never thought I'd be in the hospitality arena. You just never know, and while that uncertainty can be hard to digest without the experience to believe in a positive outcome, remember that we've all had bad things happen in life, but we're still here, with a new canvas every day on which to create a masterpiece.

The key is to not let an obstacle smear your palette. Let's consider a high-profile CEO when the daily news feed reveals bad press that affects company stock prices, and now she's in hot water with the board of directors. Dwelling on what happened is irrelevant because it's in the past and the event should affect only her work life, but what if she lets it affect everything else? She starts thinking the board wants her fired or they're bringing in a new CEO or all manner of other manufactured maladies, incubated by an insecure mind that thinks the worst.

Or maybe you get in a car accident and beat yourself up about it. "If only I'd have left five minutes later or taken the back road instead of the boulevard." We always think about the what-if and should've-done-this, but it's all just wasted energy because we can't change what already happened. It won't help to call your friend and moan for a half hour about the accident or replay the event in your head so much that you're not your fun, jovial self because your mind has the fence up.

If you stopped drinking but had a bad day and poured a couple of shots, your momentum is gone, and if tomorrow is another bad day, why not have another shot? Or you blow off the gym one day and decide it's easy enough to skip another day too. COVID was the perfect example in my world. I never should have let that derail my fitness goals; in fact, I should have been even more motivated, but I just thought, "The world sucks, so I guess I can suck too." Internal consolations allow one obstacle to turn into many more, and that's when win-the-moment bracelets come to the rescue again by not allowing a bad day to affect everything else. Change the script and redirect that energy toward something that deflates the obstacle and creates positive movement forward.

Think about the last time you had a really great day. Hopefully you're having one now! That *vibrant* feeling makes you a better employee, friend, and partner, and you waltz through the day with good vibrations. I remember a time I was on a dedicated track, taking care of my health and doing all the things I wanted to do, and met a buddy at 6:00 a.m. on a Saturday to shoot hoops. He showed up, and I was revved with energy. "You ready to do this and have an amazing day?" He looked at me and said, "What the hell is wrong with you? How are you always in such a good mood?"

I told him I don't have a secret recipe for happiness; I just love life, and that makes it easy to approach every day on a high. But I couldn't bring that same energy if I wasn't doing other great things. If I had stayed up late drinking and watching movies, I couldn't have had that same early Saturday interaction.

I debated a similar happiness-success scenario with another friend. I asked him, "If a dude wants to live on the beach and surf every day, who's to say he isn't any more successful than you?" There's no way for an outsider to know if that person is truly successful and happy. I like the surfer-and-stockbroker analogy to illustrate this. Put pictures of a surf bum and stockbroker on the wall, and ask which you think is happier with their success. Odds are most of us would select the stockbroker. But what if we list their aspirations beneath the photos? They could look like this:

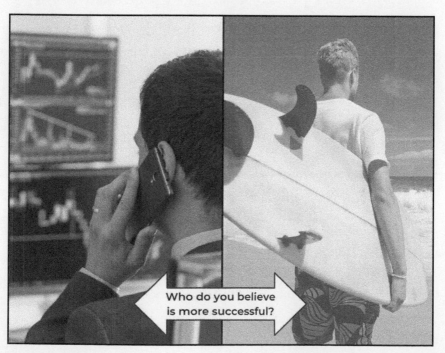

Who do you believe is more successful?

Surf bum: I just want to surf every day.

Stockbroker: I just want to surf every day.

Who's happier with their success now?

Placing preconceived belief or judgment on what makes people happy often only saps more energy. We see things other people have and think they're happy when in fact they might be miserable and the "happy things" aren't really what they wanted. In the end, we tell ourselves we should have X without defining it or should want it because someone else told us we should. Never chase someone else's goal or society's vision of success. Sadly, so many people don't genuinely enjoy what they're doing. They go to work to provide for their families and rationalize it with "This is the rat race; it's the game we have to play," but it's not. Is that job really where you want to be? If it is, that's fabulous, but today more than ever, you can do anything you want. Start a YouTube channel reviewing Pokémon cards or the latest makeup trend. The opportunities for wealth today are limited only to your imagination and motivation. I'd much rather be doing something I love and be happy in it than doing something I can hardly tolerate and making wheelbarrows of money. Don't attach success to money. You don't need a million dollars to have a great life. There are myriad spectrums of happiness in far smaller dollar amounts that people often fail to see.

The Five-Dollar Moment

When faced with an obstacle, what do new opportunities look like? How do they manifest in front of you? When my wife and I moved back to St. George, at the start of a challenging financial time when I was launching my financial practice, we had a really tight budget: the familiar scenario of keeping spending low and watching every penny to make ends meet. One day, Meagan went over her monthly budget by five dollars. As I was reviewing our budget, I called Meag to ask, "What are you doing? We don't have any extra money; why did you go over your budget?"

I was in my office, and the conversation devolved into a back-and-forth about our woes. I was facing an array of obstacles and struggling with a bout of self-doubt, but I kept showing up at work every day, determined to turn things around. A few days later, Breck called and asked me to take over as CFO of his company. We had adjacent offices at the time, and it turned out he overheard my conversation with Meagan and knew if I understood money in five-dollar increments, I'd be a perfect addition to his team. I had no idea in the moment, but not backing down from that financial obstacle created an unforeseen opportunity. Five dollars inspired a purpose and changed my life.

Humans need purpose, and I believe when you have that, obstacles are far less impactful. If you set a goal to run a mile today and you trip and fall and scrape your knee, you'll still run the mile because that's the intended purpose. However, if you're just on a leisurely jog and succumb to that same injury, odds are you are just going to turn it in and call it quits. You didn't define a purpose. With a destination in mind, an obstacle is temporary—you've defined where you want to be, what you want to do. It's a Big Hairy Audacious Goal, and you may or may not achieve it, but it's your North Star and something worth shooting for.

How does that work when most of us are on autopilot, with daily routines that are predictable and often mundane? The only sure way to fulfillment is to break that ritual, become aware, and be in charge of your decisions. Awareness is so powerful in so many different aspects of life. Being aware of what is happening around you and what your behaviors are like channels an entirely new level of strength and determination in you that you may not even realize. Don't let anyone or anything else suck you in to a loop of perpetual obstacles. Be realistic—obstacles are still going to happen, but don't let them stop you.

From Obstacles Bloom Opportunity

Think about the last time you overcame an obstacle. You felt stronger on the other side, didn't you? And more often than not, beating the obstacle created a new opportunity to embrace that wasn't there before. Even better, this scenario starts when we're kids. The other day, my daughter didn't do well at a school spelling bee, and she felt terrible, but it was a growth opportunity. I explained to her that if she wants different results next time, she must have different actions.

If she truly wants to be better at spelling, then we must put in extra work and practice every day. I let her know if she uses that terrible feeling as fuel and motivation to keep working at it every day, soon she won't have to experience the feeling again. Life never stops, and it's full of obstacles, but you will *always* come out on the other side.

How to Get There

The relationship between obstacles and opportunity is about being present. We can live only one minute, hour, day at a time, and while there might be an obstacle too big to solve in this moment, forward momentum can start immediately. I gained forty-nine pounds since COVID started, and I certainly can't lose that much today, but I can adopt healthy habits right now, and that will create opportunities to overcome the larger obstacle. Use your win-the-moment bracelets as a guide, and take one step at a time.

Your Winning Moment

Whatever the size, shape, and severity of an obstacle, acknowledging and addressing it wins the moment. When you reach the other side of a tough spot, take some time to appreciate the work you put in and let yourself feel the win. Celebrate it, and be thankful you arrived at a new and positive space. We don't always have to be moving forward every minute of the day, but when good things happen, grab those moments, hold on tight, and enjoy yourself!

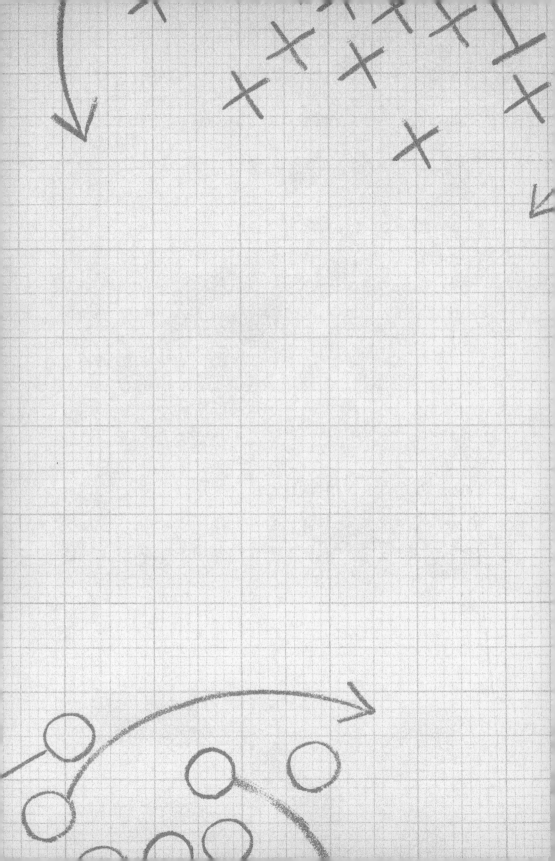

CHAPTER EIGHT

GET UNCOMFORTABLE

*The more you seek the uncomfortable, the
more you will become comfortable.*
—CONOR MCGREGOR

I have a friend who is petrified of public speaking in virtually any form. Oral reports in grade school history class spawned mumbles and shaky hands that made his speech flutter like maple leaves. He was captain of the track team, but inspiring pep talks were more like "follow me, and let's run fast." The mere thought of walking onto a stage in a packed auditorium gives him cold sweats and wobbly knees. He is uncomfortable in that sort of environment, to say the least, and avoided such terrifying scenarios at all costs. Fast-forward a few decades, and he's still likely to duck out the back door if it means escape from oral anguish. Does it matter in the grand scheme if his job doesn't require addressing large groups or he isn't giving keynote speeches at industry conventions? Probably not, but is he growing? Stretching his comfort zone?

How about you? Are you comfortable or reaching a bit further and making it hurt a little? Our natural inclination is the former, to be like water and live a life of least resistance. It's certainly a hell of a lot easier, like in my friend's case, to sit in the audience than to stand up there and conjure oratory glory that captivates a thousand people. Is that the best choice? You might feel content when everything is easygoing and following a manageable, predictable pace, and there's nothing wrong with that path, but remember, that is where you'll stay—in a manageable and predictable place.

I'm not knocking a life that maintains a familiar trajectory day in and day out; it works for a great many people. However, a side effect is becoming *too* comfortable. In fact, comfort as a daily ingredient often leads to general boredom, restlessness, a lingering "averageness," and a life that's about as exciting as watching commercials. The alternative can change your life, but it means making a dedicated shift from your same ole. It starts by breaking the habit of avoiding uncomfortable things and boils down to a very simple formula: you need to be uncomfortable in order to grow. I like to use the example of exercise, whether you train for competition or walk around the block twice a week. The only way you improve is by making it harder, pushing past your comfort zone. If you're hitting the weight room at the gym, you have to add a few extra reps or a heavier weight for your muscles to grow. A new personal record in a 5k won't happen if you just keep doing the same workout; you need to run past your usual pain threshold. Riding your bike five miles or a hundred, whatever your benchmark, requires significant sweating and days you don't even want to be out there.

The same thing happens at work. Early in my sales career, running my marketing company selling the *Wall Street Journal* at makeshift booths at BYU football and Houston Astros games and other pro events, I quickly learned that what defines a salesperson is creating opportunities that don't otherwise exist. Sure, I could just stand there on the stadium concourse and wait for someone to walk up, and I might make a few sales.

But what counts is being uncomfortable and pushing the envelope to make something bigger happen. If a guy walks by on the way to get pizza and a beer and sees me at the table, he'll keep right on walking unless I jump in with a big smile—

What counts is being uncomfortable and pushing the envelope to make something bigger happen.

"Hey, how's it going? Where are you from? Do you like the game so far?" With some engaging conversation and willingness to embrace discomfort, before long I'm making another sale. Sometimes you have to be a little outrageous, do something different.

This applies to your mental side too (without the sweating). Decades of research by experts around the world tell us that exercising our brains is as important as bench presses and cardio. That doesn't mean you need to study molecular physics on the weekends or read the collected works of Aristotle and Hemingway. Try the harder crossword puzzle, start writing a book, break out that old Rubik's Cube. Choose something that ignites your brain receptors to stimulate a new cognitive element and usher in an exciting future.

Combining physical and mental challenges cultivates a creative resilience that allows you to handle traditionally anxious moments. Perhaps you're avoiding a difficult conversation with your partner or children. Or a key employee made a blunder that hurt the company and needs a delicate face-to-face meeting. You need to come clean with something you've kept hidden for years. In examples like these and so many others, breaking down your discomfort barrier is when growth happens.

Expect, plan for, and embrace discomfort, and then harness its power to break through whatever barriers held you back from being a better you, with a previously undiscovered strength to reshape routine. One of the best parts of this? When you get used to meeting and beating unpleasant moments, your comfort zone's boundaries swell, and pretty soon you're comfortable with discomfort! Think about what that could mean: with anything that trips you up, from nervousness to act or reluctance to change, you now have the where-withal and confidence to come out on top.

One of my employees, Dres, had a procrastination tendency with certain things. When a huge hospitality project took hold here in Utah, I asked him to pull together key data points and connect with local properties to help best position our company to land the partnership. The task was uncomfortable to him for whatever reason, and it took months to get done. But in a night-and-day switch, he orchestrated a critical save at our visitor center that had sustained substantial flood damage, securing an array of contractors and ensuring the work was completed in time to get the facility back on track. He dialed in his confidence with a past challenge to instill a new relationship with discomfort. Success and failure aren't always a reflection of our ability or know-how; they're often a reflection of willingness and effort to accomplish what's in front of us.

I battle with a similar mental tug-of-war, and it happened again just the other day, sitting on my couch at home, surrounded by all the trappings of an amazing life. If you told me at eighteen years old that my world would look like this today, I would have said, "Hell, yeah," and danced a little jig. I'm CFO of a company managing over $15 million and counting in annual revenue and partnered with some of the country's most luxurious and respected hospitality groups. My team is currently at the front of building a pair of ten-thousand-plus-square-foot office and commercial spaces. I live in my dream home and drive my dream car, and I'm a published author. I don't think many people would argue that things look plenty comfortable and all of this should make me feel incredible, but I sat there thinking, Damn, why don't I feel successful?

Part of it is because I'm not working hard enough and letting society's vision of success get in the way of my own. I'm not going into each day doing uncomfortable things, but I'm feeling uncomfortable in a perceived success. I got to where I wanted to be, and now I'm maintaining it, but I can't stay in this place forever without stretching myself and actively pursuing growth. Even in the midst of writing this book, I could have done a better job. I went on vacation with my family and chose not to take advantage of downtime to review chapters and refine ideas. It's certainly not uncomfortable to read through a manuscript, but it's a hell of a lot more enjoyable to sit on the beach with a piña colada. One byproduct of that decision was feeling like a nobody in society's grand scheme—who wants to read my stuff anyway? That's the time to turn directly into the storm.

There is a great quote by Jon Acuff, "Don't compare your beginning to someone else's middle, or your middle to someone else's end. Don't compare the start of your second quarter of life to someone else's third quarter."[10]

We are all on our own journey with our destinations in mind. Technology makes it easy to compare, but we never know what stage the person we are comparing with is in. Don't waste energy focusing on someone else's success or failure; instead, harness that energy for your own.

---

10   Jon Acuff, goodreads, accessed September 22, 2022, https://www.goodreads.com/quotes/7194163-don-t-compare-your-beginning-to-someone-else-s-middle-or-your.

Intentionally Uncomfortable

It might not sound like an appealing strategy, but I encourage you to seek every opportunity to be uncomfortable. Go into the day inflated with energy and confidence, and hunt down challenging scenarios like a bloodhound. I give this advice to my sales team, and it absolutely applies to any workplace or general life situation: if you go through a full day without being uncomfortable, you didn't grow. This can be tied to dollars-and-cents growth, notching a fitness milestone, finally saying hello to your attractive classmate, or simply getting up a half hour earlier this week.

Think about an average day in your life—you expect your home to be at a comfy temperature, and the lights turn on, water comes out of the faucets, there's food in the fridge, your car starts, and so on. You'd only have to leave to go to work and make enough money to keep all of that happening, but there's so much more to life than just surviving. It's about living intentionally and with a purpose, whatever it might be. Just remember that being uncomfortable, and growing through it, is part of realizing every ounce of your potential.

The key is to recognize small changes before they turn into big ones. Life is meant to be enjoyed, and in order to enjoy it, you can't be stagnant. We are not conditioned to be stagnant, but it's easy to fall into the same routine rut, day after day. But what happens when you have a bad day? You think, Well, it was just a bad day, and then you have a bad week, bad month, bad year. It's like if a plane leaves Los Angeles bound for New York and veers just a few degrees south, it will end up way off course in Miami. Life is the same way. It might not seem like a big deal to have "just a couple" of donuts every week, but then two years goes by, and you've gained fifteen pounds. A seemingly insignificant shift in direction over a long period makes a big difference.

Our VP of sales, Spencer, is a CrossFit fanatic (you know this because he tells you about it) and mentioned one day that he got in the habit of having a glass of whiskey or two after dinner, and before he knew it, he started skipping his morning gym routine. He didn't have those evening drinks with the intention of bailing on the workouts, but when the next morning came around, he just didn't feel up to it. His whiskey and workouts were directly related, and a related example of living intentionally would be choosing to skip the drinks because morning exercise is important to him. It comes down to making deliberate decisions to achieve what you want to achieve, stay in control of your life, and not simply go along for the ride.

So, what's the best way to approach uncomfortable situations? Whether it's evening drinks or public speaking or pushing your physical limits, moments will come when you need to make intentional decisions, and how you perform when faced with adversity is a measure of what you can accomplish. This isn't always easy, given we humans are internally conditioned to survive and

How you perform when faced with adversity is a measure of what you can accomplish.

our brains want us to be safe and comfortable, not too hot or cold or hungry or tired, and that's the struggle we have to fight. When you wake up in the morning and want to head to the gym, your mind is saying, "No, stay here. The bed is warm and comfy and safe. We don't need to get all sweaty and ramp up our heart rate." And there you are, faced with a battle of which is stronger, your conscious or subconscious self.

Here's the kicker: Our subconscious minds drive a lot of our decisions, like how and when to breathe and the ability to write or walk down the street. Even when we're driving, the subconscious leads the way. We don't consciously think, Okay, I'm going to veer right here, slow down on the curve, or speed up to pass that truck. It all happens autonomously, and unless you make a determined effort to use your conscious mind, it doesn't see a lot of action. In the end, one of the best ways to manage discomfort is to flex the conscious mind. It's sort of like a gamification of life, where you intentionally decide to be in control and live with purpose.

Winning with Grace

When I ran my one and only full marathon, every participant had their own ambitions and expectations. Some maintained a strict diet of all things healthy and trained like Olympians to win the race. Others wanted to nail a specific time, and many just wanted to finish it. My goal was to finish in five hours or less, and I did it. I crossed the line in 1,500th place or something, far from record pace, but I didn't give a shit who won or what their time was. That wasn't my ambition. I was happy with my performance and glad I did the run. But what about the second-place finisher? If his or her goal was to win and they "only" took second, is that a loss? Hell no. You can be disappointed because you fell short of your goal, but second place is still a win. You just ran 26.2 miles, a tremendous accomplishment in its own right, and making the podium is something to be proud of.

And as a humorous aside, second and third place earned a spot in Jerry Seinfeld's pantheon of stand-up laughs. Telling the crowd how he enjoys the Olympics, Seinfeld talked about track-and-field athletes dedicating their lives to training—"I worked out my entire life. I never had a date, I never had a drink, I did push-ups since I was a fetus"—and then missing the gold by a hundredth of a second. In a hilarious photo finish demonstration, Seinfeld replays how winning by a nose makes the difference between "greatest guy in the world" and "never heard of him."

Back at my marathon, let's say the race winner showboated on the top step, waving their medal around and talking trash to the other runners and gloating to anyone within earshot. Beyond a demonstration of bad taste, that person missed a golden opportunity to win with grace, to celebrate a victory with respect to the event and everyone who was a part of it. In winning on any level, how you do it impacts everyone around you and influences your future performances and relationships.

When I gave lectures at our local college, I could've swaggered into the room and told all kinds of stories about how Vibrant is a badass machine that never fails and it's the best thing to ever hit the hospitality scene, or I could share our reality. That we struggle all the time to reach success points and then can't grow anymore by doing the same things, and we fail for a bit until we figure it out and work like hell to get back on top. I share with the students that we were $11.37 away (our business account's dwindling dregs) from closing our doors. It's not always enjoyable to tell tales like that, but everyone can relate to losing. As a role model, you can boast about how great everything is, but chances are the audience will tune out and think the opposite of what you intended: "I don't want to be rich and successful if it means being a pompous ass." Unfortunately, society has created a label that wealthy people are evil and selfish, and that influences others' views of and desire for success.

With that, one takeaway I always liked to leave my students with is that we often learn more in losses than wins because we don't appreciate and learn to lose. Learning to lose is a critical skill set, one that I see developing (very slowly) with my daughter. We play Guess Who? a lot, and I don't let her win because she's going to lose in life much more than winning. If I make it easy for her to beat me all the time, it takes away the value and appreciation of winning. She also needs to learn how to handle her emotions in a loss; so far, she still throws herself onto the beanbag chair and throws crying fits. To me, it's important to learn to lose at age eight rather than eighteen and derail her emotional state.

Part of the problem, once again, is society's fear of offending anyone. School and club sports leagues live by the "there's no first place" rule and hand out participation trophies like candy at a parade. My daughter's report card is all just numbers now. Her teachers don't grade with the A–F scale anymore, and I think they are doing children a disservice; an A on a project or overall class grade is something tangible to shoot for, and if you don't even try or turn in poor work, you should know that just the same. If you're good at losing, you'll be great at and comfortable with winning!

Get Uncomfortable

It can seem counterintuitive, and downright scary sometimes, but one of the best ways to grow in life is busting out of your comfort zone. It's more than just the cliché "thinking outside of the box." This is getting to know being uncomfortable and, in fact, seeking opportunities that traditionally make you nervous or uncertain of your ability to accomplish a task or attain a goal, no matter how small. Day in, day out is fine, but it's average. You're not average. Harness your conscious mind's power to embrace your potential to change struggle to opportunity.

In the space below, I'd like you to write down the top three things that, for whatever reason, you avoided today or every day or your whole life. Look that over, assess how you've traditionally handled it, and change it!

_____

_____

_____

_____

_____

_____

_____

_____

_____

How to Get There

We all know the person we want to be and know the things we're not doing that we want to do. Make sense? What are some things you could do today that you've put off because they make you feel uncomfortable? Over the course of a day, most of us are cognizant of what inspires discomfort, and the tendency is to back away. "I have to do X, but I don't want to, so I'll go the other way." Instead of turning away, use your win-the-moment bracelets as motivation to lean *in* to being uncomfortable instead of leaning out.

My wife makes amazing dinners for us nearly every night. It's a lot of work and creates stacks of cookware and measuring cups and other kitchen flotsam. For the most part, she doesn't like making dinner because that means cleaning all the dishes. I started pitching in to help, even though I hate doing dishes. I'd much rather sit on the couch and watch basketball, but I know if I make it easier for her, it's better for all of us. I just have to consciously choose to do it, and the best part is that once we choose to lean in to something uncomfortable, it creates other good things. Doing the dishes inspired me to clean the living room, and then I picked up the backyard, and before I knew it, I'd had a superproductive evening. Not only that, my son saw me helping and said, "Dad, can I help?" Priceless.

Remember that you're only uncomfortable in the moment of making a decision. Once you dive into the task, you realize it's pretty great and good things come of it. For me, the worst part of going to the gym is choosing to go. Once I get there and start working out, I love it.

Your Winning Moment

Much of the process of evolution is based on discomfort. From earliest man to millions of wildlife species, they all evolved by essentially being uncomfortable about something—habitat, food, predatorial instinct, shelter. And through all manner of discomfort comes growth, getting closer to the person you want to be. Remember that a big part of being uncomfortable is thinking you can't do something right, like people feel they need to be fit before going to the gym, but you can't get fit without going to the gym. Ultimately, it's about turning your flywheel in a direction that creates positive momentum.

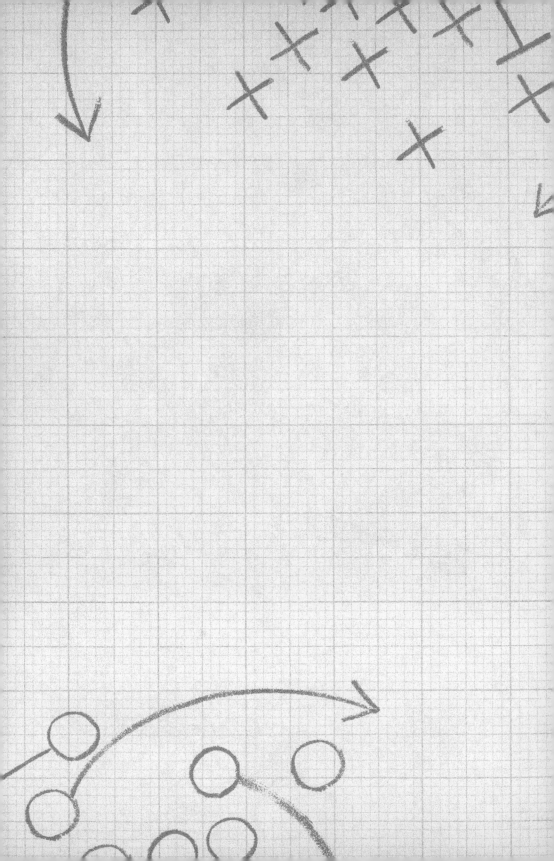

CHAPTER NINE

FIND YOUR WHY

*The two most important days in your life are the day
you are born and the day you find out why.*

—MARK TWAIN

Why?

One word with the power to change your life. Finding your why is one of the most important elements to creating a fulfilled life, and it's something you need to establish in order to live intentionally. So many things in life are challenging and difficult, but the why makes the doing worth it. If you haven't already found it or don't know what it is, I want you to find your why. It will change your life.

It changed mine. I can look to every significant moment and see how knowing my why allowed me to accomplish a goal, work through a tough situation, or simply maintain a confidence that I can do anything I set my mind to. I was already living my why the first time I came across Simon Sinek's TED talk "How Great Leaders Inspire Action." Sinek is a prolific author and renowned inspirational speaker, and his message is a great source of inspiration. I highly recommend setting aside fifteen minutes to listen to Simon's presentations or read his books. It is with this motivation that I've rebounded from setbacks or outright dismissing of goals. For example, anytime I haven't had a defined why and tried going to the gym regularly or living a healthier lifestyle, it never stuck. I've gained and lost more than forty pounds twice in the past and am now on the journey of doing it a third time. What gives? I shouldn't be swinging back and forth like a grandfather clock pendulum.

The first time this happened, my buddy Mike inspired me with his own revelation. He stayed at my house when we worked together in Arizona and one morning walked down the stairs looking like he'd seen a ghost. "I just stepped on your scale for the first time since I can remember. I don't know how I let this happen to myself. I've got to make a change." He flew back to Albuquerque that night and reported in the next morning that he had done push-ups and gone on a walk. He followed it up the next day with a similar exercise routine. The day after that, he let me know he had found and started the Insanity workout regimen, sixty days of intense training alongside a targeted diet plan.

At the time, my wife and I had also let ourselves fall into unhealthy habits, and Mike's journey motivated us. I also wanted to be healthier, more fit, and back to a somewhat athletic version of myself. I had my why, and that gave me the strength to accomplish my goals and do the hard work it takes. The issue, however, was I thought my why was only about getting back to a healthier place, not living a healthy lifestyle every day. For that reason, I eventually put the weight back on and had to start the journey all over again a few years later, with a new why that I had established and embraced.

It was then that I realized a dichotomy of sorts. I have always accomplished my professional goals because I had a firmly recognized why with a deep purpose. I wanted to be successful in any career endeavor and viewed accompanying hard work as a necessary and fulfilling component. In fact, through all the times in my life when I had to work my ass off, I was able to do it, and still do, because of my why—to provide my family a fulfilled life and create a personal legacy.

I would never let a cycle like weight fluctuation happen at work, so I created a diet-exercise chart to hold myself accountable and reach my goal. That life chapter inspired this book to share working concepts and help a larger audience live the life they desire. The bracelets were my idea of bringing those concepts to life with a constant visual reminder—it's like wearing your why on your wrist.

I have no idea if you have a why or realize what it should or could be. That is not for me or anyone else to determine. It's up to you. Take the time to dive deep into your why. Make it meaningful, with a lifelong purpose. When your winning moments reflect your why, you will be well on the way to living a life to be proud of.

> *Take the time to dive deep into your why. Make it meaningful, with a lifelong purpose.*

Purpose to Promise

Working hard for something we don't care about is called stress.
Working hard for something we love is called passion.
—SIMON SINEK

I spent my early career in sales coaching roles with teams of four to one hundred, and the most important conversation I had with them was about their why. Why are you here? Why are you doing this job? Understanding their why made it easier and more effective to coach, and by helping them accomplish their why, I never failed to reach mine.

If you're in the doldrums of life or going through the motions at a job you don't care about, it breeds stress like mosquitoes in summer. But if you love what you're doing and know that job helps provide for your family, it doesn't feel like a gulag. The why of your day-to-day is what makes your world go round, and even mundane tasks take on new light. In the midst of an intense exercise regimen to lose weight and regain a healthy lifestyle, I have to get out of bed at 7:00 a.m. every day, something I couldn't do without a deeper purpose. The why gives me motivation and infuses an appreciation of something I generally didn't have in the past.

The same kind of inspiration drives my professional life as well. Our company is in its fourth year, and we're really hitting our stride, with some exciting growth opportunities. There's a lot of work to do, and there are deadlines, expectations, and client-satisfaction demands, but it never feels stressful. Those are all necessary elements to creating an intentional, desired life.

We spend most of our adult lives at work, and life is way too short to grumble about your job on the way there, tolerate it all day, and mope because you have to do it again tomorrow. Even if you abhor "only" eight hours a day and love the rest of your life, you're losing out on so much happiness. In fact, a 2016 study "showed a lower risk of death for participants with a high sense of purpose in life. After adjusting for other factors, mortality was about one-fifth lower for participants reporting a strong sense of purpose. That's a 20 percent chance of living a longer life, simply by adopting a sense of purpose."[11] Celebrated German philosopher Friedrich Nietzsche's views followed the same path: "He who has a why can endure any how. Knowing your *why* is an important first step in figuring out

---

11   Randy Cohen et al., "Purpose in Life and Its Relationship to All-Cause Mortality and Cardio-vascular Events: A Meta-Analysis," *Journal of Biobehavioral Medicine*, vol. 78, no. 2 (March 2016), 122-33.

how to achieve the goals that excite you and create a life you enjoy living (versus merely surviving!). Indeed, only when you know your 'why' will you find the courage to take the risks needed to get ahead, stay motivated when the chips are down, and move your life onto an entirely new, more challenging, and more rewarding trajectory."[12]

Knowing your purpose allows a clear vision of what you need to do, like business writer John C. Maxwell's take on how the why influences the journey: "Dreams require down payments. Dreams are free, but the journey isn't. There is a price to pay. When you find your why you'll find your way. When you develop your will you will embark on your way. Many people start; few people finish. Many people have a dream; few people achieve their dreams."[13] Finding your why might be what it takes to chase down that new job you've always wanted, lock in a healthy diet, ignite a relationship. And this ties back to the universe's guidance. Without a clearly established why, it's impossible for the universe to provide support; you have to define where you want to go and who you want to be, and then stick with it. It's easy to take a day off from your why, and that compounds into two, then three, and then it's a week, a month, a year. If you're not actively working every day at building the life you want, you won't have it.

Consider the end of Maxwell's quote, that many people have a dream but few people achieve it. Were their dreams realistic? When my sister said she wanted to be financially free but didn't know what that meant, she was mired in a nebulous space that, if left unattended, would see her stuck in an endless spin cycle. History is full of similar stories. Before the Wright brothers proved otherwise, it was unrealistic to think a metal object with an engine could fly. Electricity wasn't realistic.

---

12   Dr. Margie Warrell, "Do You Know Your 'Why?' 4 Questions To Find Your Purpose," October 30, 2013, https://www.forbes.com/sites/margiewarrell/2013/10/30/know-your-why-4-questions-to-tap-the-power-of-purpose/?sh=b99701473ad3.

13   John C. Maxwell, AZ Quotes, accessed September 22, 2022, https://www.azquotes.com/quote/798185.

Walking on the moon certainly wasn't something we thought possible. But it's important to remember that having an unrealistic dream isn't a problem; you just need to realize why you want that dream.

Let's say you want to live in a mansion. Why? What is the purpose behind that dream? What is living in a mansion going to do for your life? When people take the time to really dissect their lives and what is important to them, internalize beliefs and thoughts of what matters, it inspires achievable goals with deep meaning, and that provides the motivation to go get them. Take my weight-loss ups and downs, for example. If I just said I didn't want to be overweight anymore but didn't make daily changes to make it happen, it shows I don't genuinely want that dream. When former employees of mine proclaimed they wanted to be a manager but often showed up late to work, I said, "You don't really want to be a manager."

"What do you mean? Of course I do."

"You think you want to be a manager because it seems logical to want the next higher position with responsibility and power. On the surface, that seems like something you want, but you can't make it to work on time now. You need to show me you deserve the role today."

Your actions must be aligned with your words. If they aren't, your dreams are just fluff. It's like crying wolf—if you keep saying you want to do something but never do it, eventually your audience will stop supporting you, and that support is critical to help accomplish your goals. Patience is also a key element. Dreams take time, and you have to put in the work, whether it's a lifetime career achievement or short-term aspiration like my weight loss. I know I can't lose forty pounds this week, and some weeks will be better than others; I just have to keep putting in the work. Some weeks, I might not lose any weight, or even gain another pound or two, but I'll break through that obstacle and keep moving forward.

Here's another example: My office colleague, Allie, wanted to get a real estate license. Her father is a highly successful businessman with an armload of real estate deals that happened organically through various projects. He wanted Allie to be part of the commission, so she decided to dive fully into the game. She was super motivated, studied every day, and failed the test the first time. She hasn't been back to try again since then, even though her dad continued to tally more lucrative deals. She kept avoiding scheduling another test out of fear of failing again and sour grapes of missing out on past commissions.

I encouraged her not to stop. "If you really want to do this, don't wait. The longer you wait, the harder it will be to pass, and every day, it's a bigger burden to bear. There's nothing you can do about deals that already happened. But right now you can retake the test and move forward. Once you get your license, you're set to go." With that kind of mental-behavioral trajectory, you eventually reach a point where you don't want to try anymore, but that's when you stop and ask, Did I really want it in the first place? If the answer was yes, you'd get it done. In Allie's story, even setting a new test date was uncomfortable because her subconscious didn't want to fail. She didn't really want to retake that test; it was her dad's goal, not hers. Clarify your dream and bring it to life, and your chances of succeeding are exponentially higher.

Know Your Ikigai

The Japanese concept of *ikigai* dates back many thousands of years, and its powerful meaning is just as poignant today. A blend of the terms *iki*, meaning "alive" or "life," and *gai*, meaning "benefit" or "worth," *ikigai* is what gives your life worth, meaning, or purpose—your why.

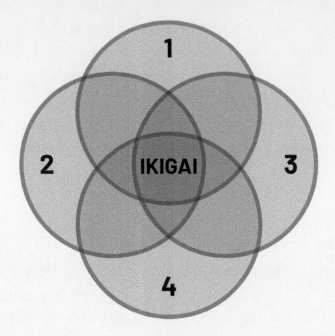

1. What you love
2. What you are good at

3. What the world needs
4. What you can be paid for

I identify strongly with *ikigai* and what it stands for, and the above graphic is a powerful visual representing what we can accomplish with a firm understanding of self-worth. Sadly, many people can't identify with it or understand what it means, and that can lead to self-sabotage, anxiety, fears, and self-doubt. I remember one afternoon when my daughter walked into my office at home, her face colored sad. I asked what was wrong, and she mumbled, "I'm stupid."

I didn't expect a comment like that but was quick to rein it in. "Liv, would you let someone call your mom stupid? Or say something mean about your brother, or me?"

"No."

"Then why are you saying it about yourself? Your mind and body are internalizing that, and when your teacher asks you a question in school, your reaction will be to think you're stupid, and that takes away your ability to succeed. You've told yourself a negative thing, and your body bears the stress of it. You cannot say negative things about yourself, or they will stick with you and come true."

She was only eight years old at the time, but my pep talk clicked, and I got smiles out of her. If you say you can't have that dream or can't make that goal or all manner of self-deprecating words and behaviors, failure is almost always the result.

Would your eight-year-old self be proud of who you are today? If you could time machine back and show your kid self what he or she would become, would the little you be excited or say, "I don't want to do that or be like that"? Of course, as kids we don't have life's burdens weighing us down; we're just full of joy and have fun and goals at the time that are about doing things we love. But if the answer from the young you was no, you'd have to make a change. And you can still make changes today, with the understanding that you are capable of doing anything you want to. Once you have your why, nothing can stop you.

Best of all, you can have more than one why, and they can evolve every day or twice a month or six times a year. You can have a new why with every life chapter. You can have fewer or more; there is no set-in-stone prescription. There are, however, some tried-and-true tools to help discover your why. Here are a handful that have inspired me:

➡ Discover what makes your life more fulfilling.

➡ Think of a moment when time didn't matter or you didn't even notice it.

➡ What activities from your childhood did you enjoy most?

➡ What types of things do people ask you for help with?

➡ If your time on earth was limited, what would you be doing?

➡ What kind of work would you do for free?

➡ If money didn't matter, what would you do for work?

I think of it as being like an onion. You have to get a few layers in to see what you're made of. I followed a similar approach with my former cellular staff when they struggled with sales. I asked what they thought was going on but assured them my inquiry wasn't about sales quotas; it was discovering what they were working for. If one of them needed extra money for a car repair, for example, we looked at the real-time situation: Your commission is X, you need Y to fix the car, and there are seven days left in the month. How much commission per day do you need? It was like one of those high school math problems, and for that employee, it became about getting their car back, not meeting company objectives, and that made it easier for them to achieve it.

Look at the fifth point in the tools list above. Life isn't just about making it through each day and surviving until you die. If you're not enjoying life, what's the point? Every day is a gift filled with choices—you get to choose your response to everything that happens and enjoy those things or let them ruin your day. Bring an infectious energy and share it with others. Be a source of joy. And the next time someone asks why, you can confidently reply, "Because why matters."

You and Your Why

Discovering your why is about purpose. Everything you do has a purpose associated with it. Your workplace, for example, likely has a mission statement or core values. To have longevity at a company, you need to define the skills and ethics you can bring to work every day, and our personal lives are no different. Think of it as your internal mission statement, and remember that a robust, awesome why has to come from you.

How to Get There

What drives you? What do you look forward to every day? It's critical to discover and establish your why before moving on successfully and efficiently in life, but keep in mind there is no prescription for finding your why. It takes time to peel back your onion layers and dig deep, and it might entail applying a few different renditions before you truly figure it out. Take a few minutes right now and write down some ingredients of what your why could look like:

_____

_____

_____

_____

_____

_____

_____

_____

Your Winning Moment

Establishing your why initiates a litany of good things, starting with a sense of direction and life meaning. You might not like your job, but if you approach it with a greater purpose, it makes going to work more palatable and in many cases can improve your outlook and performance. Life is too short to not do something you love, and one reason I've always loved my jobs is because I never considered them as doing something for the company; I did it for me. That made me very good at my work because my mission to be successful matched the company's. With a firmly established why, the same approach can apply to your everyday life.

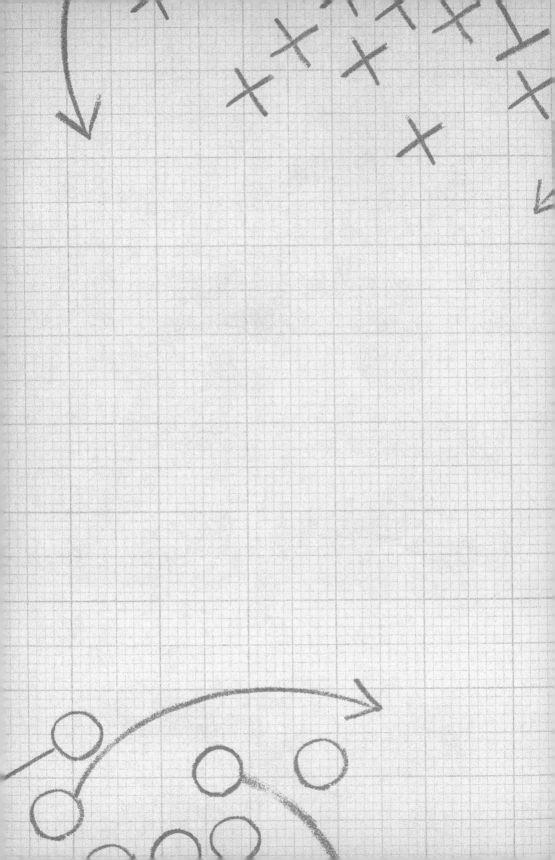

CHAPTER TEN

EMBRACE YOUR PIVOT

The moment you give up, is the moment you let someone else win.
—KOBE BRYANT

The first time I picked up a basketball, I had a blast just bouncing it around and flinging it toward the net, pacified by countless hours of the unfettered joy of a little kid. My dad often joined me, and I soon learned skills that made the game even more fun, including fundamentals like the pivot, an intentional shift to another direction to fire off a pass to a teammate or fake out an opponent prior to a Jordan-esque drive to the hoop. On the court, and in life, a well-executed pivot can inspire winning moments; you simply need to embrace your ability to make the move.

We all had the opportunity to realize pivots in recent years with COVID, the great disruptor. It has been all but impossible not to make significant personal and professional changes to maintain some semblance of normalcy—and sanity. The virus hit the hospitality industry especially hard here in Utah, forcing copious layoffs at hotels, and all my company's clients essentially said they couldn't pay us anymore. We worked for free for as long as we could, and for a while, it looked like Vibrant might not survive, following the script of so many other small businesses around the world.

At the time, an executive director position opened with Utah's Tourism Industry Association. I had some solid relationships in the industry, nailed the interview, and landed the job, offering the opportunity to continue providing for my family while still running Vibrant. After helping ignite a Utah-tourism spark that significantly enhanced state coffers, I found myself navigating a transition out of the director role, pivoting again to take advantage of every available prospect to part the veil of an uncertain future.

Looking back, I see that my entire life has been a series of pivots, none of which were expected and which were certainly not planned. In short, a pivot is an unplanned change of course. What happens next is up to you. How do you respond to the unexpected? Do you waver back on your heels, unsure which way to turn? Wage an internal fight-or-flight battle? Make a reactive decision? I believe the best way to capitalize on a pivot is being aware of the catalyst in play, be it crisis or inspiration or challenge. Crisis almost always brings clarity, and frustrating challenges can lead to the brightest of futures. Recognizing opportunities in every moment then helps establish life direction—a promising recipe for a delectable feast, if you know when to stir the pot.

One of the key ingredients of a pivot is courage. When it feels like you're treading water or need a "change of scenery" to approach a troublesome roadblock, don't be afraid to switch gears. Doing what you know best or following a traditional, seemingly comfortable, path is fine, but doing so often fosters, at the least, an average life and in many cases can spiral to additional challenges or even a space of despair.

Don't let that happen. Plant a foot, look to promise, and turn in that direction. Throughout this book, I've shared stories of personal pivot points and those of friends and colleagues. These examples are the ideal fuel to invigorate you with the power of pivot and what that can mean to a fuller, confident, intentional self.

KICKED OFF THE TEAM

When my friend Breck kicked me out of a business deal to open a mobile phone store, I took control, made some phone calls, and within the day, established a new and ultimately very successful opportunity.

INTO THE WHEELHOUSE

Over the course of one year, I transitioned from running a very small company to managing an entire district, with one hundred employees and a tremendous pivot in job responsibility that I had to learn on the go.

THE FIVE-DOLLAR CFO MOMENT

When my wife went over our monthly budget by five dollars, we spiraled into a frustrating argument. Breck overheard the conversation and a few days later offered me the CFO position at his company. I pivoted from a financial obstacle to an unplanned and life-changing opportunity.

HAPPILY EVER AFTER

When my wife discovered her individual self, with her own perspective, part of me didn't appreciate it because I thought it was easier to just do it my way. I had to realize that in our journey, neither of us would be the same person as the relationship grew, and I ultimately recognized how wonderful it was to finally walk beside each other in a place of mutual respect and understanding.

THE CHINA EFFECT

Driving to the Chinese consulate in LA when the bank called and said they were withdrawing funding. With a lifeline deal hanging in the balance to save our biggest project, we pivoted away from the would-be doomsday, stuck to our plan, and earned a resounding success.

LEAH'S SCHOOL DAZE

The time when my employee Leah realized that taking additional college courses and doing homework every night didn't make sense for her actual life purpose, and instead funneled her energy into growing her own company.

Trust Your Gut

Each of these scenarios has a common catalyst—awareness to leverage experience and relationships to create opportunity. Conversations, unexpected change, and "everyday" life moments provide the stimulus to change, moments when you're tuned in to realize, "This is it. This is the time to do it." Throughout our lives, unique and wonderful things happen when the universe comes to a place when timing and circumstance are just right. That's when you need to be aware,

Unique and wonderful things happen when the universe comes to a place when timing and circumstance are just right.

present, and ready to make a pivot. If you move too soon or too late, the opportunity won't be what it needs to be, and we know all too well that all our moments, which turn to days and weeks and years, pass by so quickly.

That's where trusting your gut comes in. I learned to do it walking into grade school. With both parents in teaching, I had a very regimented homework schedule. There was no free time or goofing with friends until all assignments were finished and, most importantly, understood. We had home-based spelling bees, and I often studied with my parents well into the evenings. Sometimes my dad asked me to spell words on the way to school, and I'd start to spell one—M-O-U-N-T-A—and then stop and change it. Dad always said, "You have to trust your gut. You were spelling it right the first time, but when you second-guess yourself, you end up getting it wrong." That guidance stuck with me my whole life because more often than not, intuition will be right, and you have to be willing to trust your instinct, even if it seems scary.

A great analogy is the stock market, where you can make or lose a great deal of money based on when you decide to pivot. Naturally, you want to buy more stock when everything's on fire, but human nature is to wait to be sure it stays that way. You won't make any money, of course, if you buy only when things are rosy and risk-free. For example, if the market is doing terribly today, I don't care because my strategy is built on a thirty-year trajectory. The market's ups and downs are irrelevant to my end game. Life is the same—we're not trying to make it to age thirty or forty; we're shooting for one hundred, and we understand the road from birth to one hundred will be littered with obstacles and challenging moments, but those obstacles are digestible when we realize they are only temporary.

Keep in mind that pivoting can be difficult. You'll shy from making a life pivot when everything is clicking along on an even keel, but many times, a veritable pot of gold waits on the other side. A friend of mine's family saw as much on a northern Wisconsin lake and a cabin born of vision and the courage to follow it. When the place went up for sale, it looked like hell and needed a lot of work, but they could see past the moldy walls and frayed plywood, sold their existing cabin, and got to work. On the solid foundation of a determined pivot, his family turned the dilapidated place into a showcase and incubator of perennial memories.

They didn't have some kind of all-knowing orchestrator guiding decisions; they followed their instinct and didn't second-guess. No one can make decisions for you as well as you can for yourself. I'm not against tapping into outside sources for inspiration and motivation, especially if you're unsure of something. But if you already know what you want or need to do, don't let anyone change that. There's a powerful strength already inside you. Let it lead the way. Sometimes you'll trust your gut, and that decision will be the wrong one, and that's okay. It creates opportunity for a different pivot. Remember that it's a lot easier to accept failure from your own decision over someone else's, and you can take appreciation in knowledge gained along the way. If you're in the wheelhouse to make the call, it creates an altogether new and dynamic life.

Pivot Points

Life isn't linear. We don't start and finish on a flat line—life is a wild, topsy-turvy roller coaster ride, and all those peaks and valleys are pivot points. We can't appreciate the view only from the top; the low points, although difficult to admire or appreciate in the moment, are just as important, and at times even more so. Instead of viewing life like a gradual, steady rise to the top, think of it as a mountain range, and like its summits, valleys are also filled with inspiration, learning, and fulfillment.

How to Get There

Give yourself a chance to be right. Your life can be any way you want it. You can wake up in the morning and choose to make the day a great one, or you can fire expletives at the alarm clock and grumble through every step. If getting up early is your kryptonite—or a perpetual challenge at work, or that last step toward a healthy diet—don't just give up or believe the grass is greener elsewhere. Dig in and pivot. Changing direction to something better inspires wins.

Your Winning Moment

Success in recognizing and embracing a pivot is when you see the next opportunity and you take it. If you're at a point where you feel the day is a real drag, make a decision. Instead of "This day just couldn't get any worse," reorient your compass. Maybe you enjoyed reading this book and learned new things but haven't done any of the exercises—make today the day you put on the bracelets and win the day.

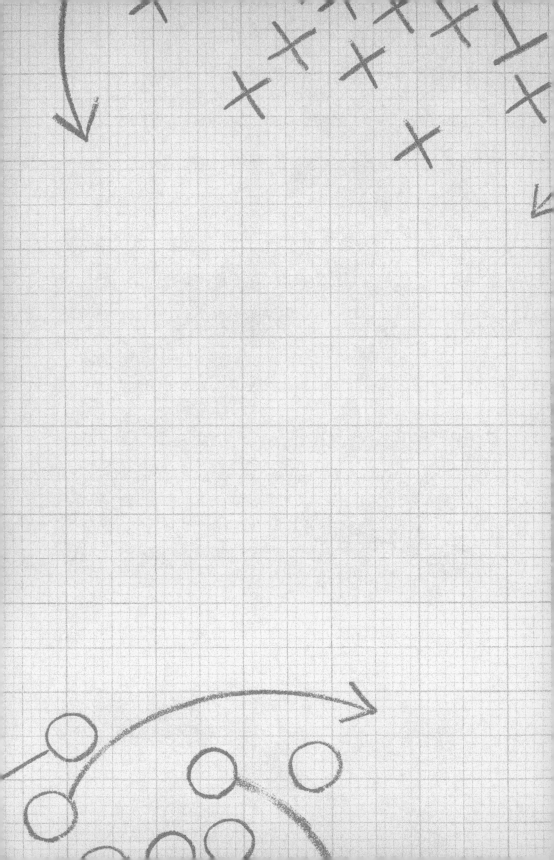

CHAPTER ELEVEN

THE MOMENT MATTERS

What do we do about the soul, since people have made such a mess out of it? "Put it on the highest of mountains!" one man says. But the people crawl up the mountains like ants, find the soul, and make it a trophy. So the wise men decree, "Put it at the bottom of the deepest seas!" But the people build underwater vessels and dive down under. They find the thing, bring it to the surface and put it in a museum. So the wise men say, "Put it beyond the farthest planet!" But the people build spacecraft and venture off and find it. They bring it back and make warfare over it. The wise men are confounded because none of them knows where to put the soul. And then one stands up and says, "I've got it! Put it in the people themselves since they never look there."

—THE FABLE OF THE WISE MEN FROM
THE WIM HOF METHOD

Y ou're going to finish reading this book today.

What happens next? When you turn the last page and close the covers, will you feel different than you did at chapter one, or will you just put this on a dusty shelf with the rest of your motivational books? Reading is learning, contentment, influence, fulfillment. One story might inspire and another create knowledge, and none of that is a bad thing. But if you read books like this one without putting their message into action and ended up with mine in your hands, you haven't taken the content to heart, and most likely you're in the same place you started.

Let's change that today. I've shared antidotes and encouragement on these pages, and now the responsibility shifts to you. Have you done the exercises? Given genuine thought to your why? Are you ready to let this book make a difference in your life? Every chapter here contains powerful, actionable content, but you don't have to adhere to it all—even just one thing sets the stage. It doesn't matter if it's winning the moment, making a pivot, finding your why, or proclaiming your destination to the universe. Choose something, identify with it, and do it *today*.

Winning alters the chemistry of your mind and boosts the odds of winning again.

I hope that through the course of this book, you've realized that winning isn't everything and it's okay to lose. In fact, in the throes of losing, we often learn more than we do in a win. But now that you know why winning matters, what are you going to do with it? As we learned with the winner effect, winning alters the chemistry of your mind and boosts the odds of winning again. However, you have to compete in order to win; you can't just sit on the sidelines. Life isn't meant to be viewed from the sidelines, watching other people win. It's meant to be played with every single ounce of ability you have.

And what happens if we give it all we have and don't always win? My most important pregame pep talk: Know that you will lose. It will happen, so get used to it, but never forget that a significant component of loss is knowledge and lessons learned. Losing is hardly a pleasant experience and can devolve into a lingering negative mindset, but if you recognize it for what it is—the whole thing sucked, I hated it, I don't ever want it to happen again—you can turn that into powerful strength going forward. In that time I lost all my money in a bad investment, it was the worst possible scenario in the moment, but it's a rare day anymore that I give that loss a second thought. It happened, it's over, so why waste energy dwelling on it? I can't change it, but I can learn from it and direct my energy toward right now.

Don't let bad stuff from yesterday or last week or last year suck away your energy for today. It has no purpose and certainly doesn't serve you in a positive light. Not only that, but it creates negative momentum. If you spend your time dwelling on loss or failure, it starts the negative wheels rolling, and now you've essentially pre-determined that everything's bad. But what if you approached it a different way?

Knowing why you lost or what contributed to it better equips you to win next time. From a job interview that went south, for example, comes knowledge to help you nail the next one. How did I answer the questions? Is my résumé dialed in? What could I have done better? Did I have food in my teeth? Ultimately, that one loss breeds confidence for a hundred wins. And you get to define what a win looks like.

I helped my wife understand this when she wrapped up thirty consecutive days of exercise. When she missed the next day, she beat herself up about ending the streak. I was surprised and asked, "Have you ever worked out thirty days in a row before?"

"No, I haven't. Not even close," she replied.

"Then why aren't you celebrating? You get to define whether today is a win or a loss, and you're choosing to mark it as a loss, even though you just accomplished something amazing." We talked about how her mind internalized a one-day "loss" as a loss for the whole month when in fact the opposite should happen (in addition to the importance of giving her body time to rest).

In another example, a friend of a friend struggles with weight far higher than he wants it to be. He doesn't have to lose thirty or twenty or even ten pounds to feel good about it. Losing just one pound is a win, and he's closer to his goal than when the day started. That's the key driver—many people give up on a goal because they think the win is at the end. If losing twenty pounds is the goal, they don't feel they've won until all twenty pounds are gone. But even five pounds, part of the ultimate goal, is a positive and moves the needle down the road.

Remember that little things matter. If your alarm clock is the bane of your day, get up before it goes off tomorrow. There's a win, and it ignites positive momentum for the rest of the day, like Jim Collins's flywheel. You don't need it to roll along at full speed right away, but once it turns in the right direction, you're accustomed to it and gravitate toward things in your life that make wins a regular occurrence.

We can find good or bad in anything, right? It's the proverbial cup half-full, half-empty mantra. How do you see the world? I remember a trip to Chicago for my dad's birthday and a choice to be miserable or live in the moment. Chicago in October comes with the city's notorious weather—cold, wind, rain, maybe snow—and we were treated to the whole lineup. Dad's birthday started with a gale blasting rain horizontally through downtown, with bursts of sleet and snow for good measure. But instead of holing up in a hotel room bitching about the weather and vowing never to set foot in that town again, we got out there and walked the streets and laughed and embraced what it feels like to live in that blustery world. We found the good and made it an unforgettable day.

That's my prescription for life. Be your own Thoreau and *experience* it—contact!—in whatever way works best for you. What's the secret to make that happen? There isn't one. Here you are, ten chapters in, and you're thinking, What the hell, he didn't give me anything I can use, and that's because there's nothing to give; you already know or have a good idea of everything I've shared in this book. The "secret" is that nothing I've shared is worth anything if you don't start. The value isn't in knowledge alone; value comes from doing. You can be the world's smartest person, but without action, knowledge is only so much dead weight, hanging around with nothing really to do. Spiritual teacher and self-help powerhouse Eckhart Tolle pointedly speaks to this idea in his straightforward, inspiring way: "Most humans are never fully present in the now, because unconsciously they believe that the next moment must be more important than this one. But then you miss your whole life, which is never not now."

If you don't agree or identify with anything in this book, I'm okay with that, but I do care that you realize that *you* are in control of your destiny and enjoyment of every day. If you don't like your job, the way you look, where you live, your car, your friends—there's no one else to blame but you, and you have the power to change your relationship with all of it. If something or someone doesn't bring you joy, remove that element from your life and replace it with whatever makes you happy, exhilarated, and content with who you are and where you want to be.

So, about that "I know nothing" proclamation I shared with you in chapter one. I do know why winning matters, and I know you have the capacity to do it. You can win every day. Go. Do. Be.

Your life will thank you for it.

ABOUT THE AUTHOR

Cody Adent grew up in the small town of Cheyenne, Wyoming. It was in Cheyenne that he developed his love for sports and started his journey of learning the power of winning and losing. Before high school, he moved to St. George, Utah, where he currently lives with his wife, two children, and two Labs. As you will learn throughout this book, Cody has always had an entrepreneurial spirit. That spirit motivated Cody's desire to skip college and head directly into the business world, creating his first business at nineteen years old.

Cody is currently the President and CFO of Vibrant Management, a hospitality management company based in St. George, Utah, with clients all over the Rocky Mountain West. Vibrant's mission is to "Create a Place Where Dreams Become Reality." They do this not just for their clients but for their team members as well. At Vibrant they build brands and digital footprints for properties that are ready to be, or about to be, industry leaders. Currently under management at Vibrant is the Cliffrose, a Hilton Curio Collection property that is the number one Hilton Curio in the world. If you want more information, go to www.thevibrantteam.com.

CONTACT

If you are interested in working with Vibrant Management you can connect with us here:

Website: www.thevibrantteam.com

Phone: 435-233-9224

Instagram: @thevibrantteam

Email: reachout@thevibrantteam.com

At Vibrant we focus on our niche, which we consider small boutique properties with 3-4 star ratings located in North America. We offer the following services:

- Full Management
- Revenue Management
- Marketing
- SEO
- Branding
- Website
- Consulting
- Graphic Design

If you are interested in working with me directly you can connect with me here:

Website: www.CodyAdent.com

Phone: 435-680-6867

Instagram: @cody_adent

LinkedIn: @CodyAdent

Twitter: @cody_adent

Email: cody@thevibrantteam.com

If you are interested in working with me directly or would like me to participate in a keynote or lecture presentation, please reach out via email as that is my most preferred method. For lectures, I'm able to speak on a wide variety of topics ranging from the contents of this book to the ins and outs of the business. We can sort out which would be the best topic or style for your event during the planning process.

NOTES